Failure is Not an Option

Failure is Not an Option

A Memoir

HYDN ROUSSEAU

FAILURE IS NOT AN OPTION
A MEMOIR

iUniverse books may be ordered through booksellers or by contacting:

iUniverse
1663 Liberty Drive
Bloomington, IN 47403
www.iuniverse.com
1-800-Authors (1-800-288-4677)

Because of the dynamic nature of the Internet, any web addresses or links contained in this book may have changed since publication and may no longer be valid. The views expressed in this work are solely those of the author and do not necessarily reflect the views of the publisher, and the publisher hereby disclaims any responsibility for them.

Any people depicted in stock imagery provided by Thinkstock are models, and such images are being used for illustrative purposes only. Certain stock imagery © Thinkstock.

ISBN: 978-1-4917-8990-2 (sc)
ISBN: 978-1-4917-8989-6 (e)

Library of Congress Control Number: 2016902495

Print information available on the last page.

iUniverse rev. date: 02/11/2016

To my mother, a strong, tough woman who made no excuses. Thank you for not giving up on me and for always pushing me to follow my dreams. Thank you for helping me to develop into a man. I dedicate this book to you! May your soul rest in peace, I love you.

Preface

My name is Hydn Rousseau. I was born in Brooklyn, New York. My parents were born in Haiti. My mother and father were both around five feet five inches tall. I don't know how my parents met, nor do I have any knowledge of their lives in Haiti.

My mother, Adeline Lopes, had five children with my father, Guy Rousseau. I have very little memory of Guy Rousseau. I always wonder what life could have been like with my father. It is a void in me that I think of from time to time.

I was never told by any of my siblings why my mother and Guy Rousseau divorced. One day we were living in New York. The next thing I knew, we moved to Florida. The first city we moved to was Miami. We lived in Miami for only a week and then moved to a town called Belle Glade. Belle Glade was approximately one hundred miles from Miami. The drive from Miami to Belle Glade was an enjoyable experience. I remember looking out the window and daydreaming. Finally we arrived in Belle Glade. The car stopped in front of an apartment building. After my mother came out of the office, we walked into an apartment.

The walls were made of concrete blocks. The restrooms and kitchen were located outside in a common area for the tenants who lived in the apartment building.

Mother struggled to make ends meet. I remember always being hungry as a child. On most days, bread and sugar water were all the family had to eat. Things were really hard on my mother. My mother could not read or write English. She depended on her children to interpret any mail or letters that she received. My sister was the point person when it came to interpreting. She was my mother's right-hand woman.

My mother began working in the fields, picking beans, oranges and cutting cane. There were not many job opportunities in Belle Glade outside of the agriculture field.

It was a beginning.

Acknowledgments

I want to thank my family for allowing me the time and space to write this book. I know that it must have been hard to tell me to go back and rewrite this book for the third or fourth time. Thank you for listening to me read the book to you each time. Although you had listened to the book and known all the contents, you listened as if it was the first time. My kids played an important part in writing this book. When I would get tired or lose focus, Jordan, Tyler, Angel, Joshua, or Warren would encourage me to keep writing. I thank my wife and kids from the bottom of my heart. Thank you!

I want to give a special shout-out to my son Tyler Williams. This book took me approximately three years to write. One of the main reasons that I rewrote the book for the fourth time was because of Tyler. Tyler was the first person to tell me to go back and rewrite the book. When I thought that the book was finished, Tyler challenged me to give more of myself to the person who would be reading the book. I dedicate the book that I am currently writing "Imprison the Mind". Tyler asked me to insert the "Action Plan," a chapters out of Imprison the Mind, into this book. *Imprison the Mind* is the current book that I am working writing. Tyler forced me to include those two chapters from the book. *Imprison the Mind* will be completed in early 2016.

Tyler Williams is fortunate to attend the best high school in the world, Oxbridge Academy. He is destined to play football in 2020. To all the schools in the country that have not given Tyler an offer, He will make you pay for it on Saturdays and eventually on Sundays. Mark my words, Tyler Williams will be inducted into the NFL Hall of Fame. Michigan State, Alabama, Oregon, and any other school that misses the opportunity to offer Tyler Williams a college scholarship will miss out on an awesome kid with tremendous power. He will prove to everyone that six foot one is tall enough to play defensive end. In one of the recent play-off games, Tyler had three sacks. You can follow Tyler Williams on Huddle. Huddle is the sport site for kids.

Special thanks go out to Evans MacDowell. Evans helped me with the initial editing of this book. Please pick up his book 905 to Rio by Evans MacDowell. I also want to thank everyone who read the book and provided feedback. Thank you!

Introduction

If you were ever told that you would not accomplish anything in this lifetime, told that you would not achieve your goals or live your dreams, if you are divorced, had no father in your life, lived in poverty, or a convicted felon trying to start a new life. This book is for you.

My father walked out on my mother and four kids when I was five years old. Most of my daily meals as a young man were bread and sugar water. I did not graduate from high school. I was convicted for selling drugs and served eight and a half years in prison. That did not stop me from accomplish my goals and dreams.

Although those things happened to me, I did not allow myself to become a victim. I did not begin blaming anyone else for my circumstance. I stop making excuses and took full responsivity for my actions. I begin taking little steps and I have overcome all of those temporary setbacks. I never gave up. I am a happily married man with four children. I have a successful business for more than ten years. I am a successful entrepreneur. I attend all of my kids' home and away games. I volunteer in my community, every summer I mentor kids through the game of basketball.

You can accomplish your goals and dreams as well! Commit yourself to reading this book to the end, and begin applying the skills you will learn reading this book in your daily life.

Thank you for giving me the opportunity to help inspire you. I hope that this book will help you to tap within the greatness within you and help you accomplish your goals and dreams. It is my honor to be a part of your life transformation.

Chapter 1

The Beginning

One day my mother called a family meeting and explained to us her plan. She told us that she needed to trust us to do the following:

1. When she left the house to go to work, we were not to go outside or open the door for anyone. If we needed to use the restroom, all of us had to go together as a group.
2. We had to share the food in the house and not eat all of the food in one day.
3. We were not to tell anyone of our struggles or what went on inside our house.
4. When we started school, we were to be there early and to come straight home when school was out. We were not to speak to anyone or make any stops along the way. Once home, we were to change clothes immediately and stay in the house.
5. We were to keep the house clean at all times.
6. We were not to speak to strangers. If anyone touched us inappropriately we were to tell her or a policeman.

We all promised Mother that we would follow her rules.

Mother woke up early the following morning, got us prepared for school, and headed off to work. My siblings began walking to school. We always arrived at school forty-five minutes before the school gate opened. We looked forward to the school meals. A hot meal before class was a great way to start the day.

I was picked on a lot in school, especially after my hair cut. Mother would always have the barber to remove all of hair on my head. My head was as shiny as glass. I wore the same clothes to school every day. My sibling and I only had one shirt and pair of pants each to wear to school. I was bullied by the popular kids in school too. The bullies would make girls slap me or take turns beating on me after school; it was humiliating and embarrassing. It was no fun going to school and being bullied and pressured. I did not know how to communicate my experiences to my siblings or teachers or mother. I did not want to disappoint my mother or appear to be a coward.

I can't imagine what my brothers and sisters went through during their school days. None of us spoke about how we were treated in school. We did not make any excuses or complain to each other. We got up every morning and went to school on time, no excuses.

Each day after school, my siblings and I went home and changed out of our school clothes. We cleaned the house and completed our homework before Mother arrived home. After our homework and chores were completed, we would either make peanut butter and jelly sandwiches or spread butter over slices of bread. We enjoyed making sugar water or Kool-Aid. Sometimes we were able to make lemonade. We would always be creative when it came to finding something to eat for the night.

My brothers and I did not have a typical life. We would look out the window and see other kids running around and having fun or playing with their toys. It was difficult watching the other kids play, but we honored the promise we made to mother and stayed inside our home.

Mother joined the family to a Catholic church located on the outskirts of town. We loved going to church. My siblings and I looked forward to going to church on Sundays. Church seemed to make mother happy. She would not miss a Sunday service unless she was sick, which was not very often.

When Mother was not working, she spent all of her time with us. We watched TV and spend a lot of time together. Mother struggle to make ends meet, and we could clearly see it, but she never complained or gave up. I did not know at the time, mother refuse apply for food stamps or take any government assistance. Mother began working harder and longer hours.

Mother's work began to pay off. Mother was able to purchase rice and meat. Things began to get better for us as a family each day. My mother's plan was slowly coming together. We were able to have more hot meals, mostly rice. We knew that when mother was beginning to earning more money. There were more hot meals on the table. We went from eating bread and sugar water to having rice and meat three or four days a week. We never gave up on the mayonnaise or butter or peanut-butter sandwiches, but we preferred having hot meals. We would always thank our mother for all of her hard work.

Mother knew she was making progress as it related to our food situation. However, our living condition had not changed. During the winter months we were extremely cold. The summer months were the worst. The walls would sweat when it was humid and the house was hot. At night, our bodies sweat and became sticky. It was difficult sleeping next to each other in the hot apartment. No one ever complained or made any excuses about our condition.

One day after church, Mom informed us that in order for her to change our living conditions, we would have to take two steps back. I did not understand my mother's logic at the time, but things went back to the way they were in the beginning when we first arrived at Belle Glade. We were no longer eating hot meals. We were back to mayo, butter, and peanut butter and jelly sandwiches. We were confused at the time, but we knew not to challenge Mother. Even though we did not know our mother's plans, we continued to keep our promise to her and follow the rules, and we kept our commitments we'd made to her at the family meeting.

Chapter 2
The Struggle Continues

I kept wondering what my mother's plan was. She was working longer hours, but we were not eating any hot meals. We knew that Mom would always do what was best for us, but we wondered what was going on.

One day, out of the blue, my sister dropped out of school and began working with mother in the fields picking beans, oranges and finally cutting cane.

We were afraid when my older sister and mother were not home. So at eight years old I took it upon myself to be the leader of the house and to keep everyone calm. I was just as afraid. I figured if I showed courage and kept a positive attitude that would keep all of us calm. My older brother was in charge at nine years old; however, I felt it was my responsibility to take the lead.

During our walks to school when we encountered danger, I would say a prayer and confront the danger. I remember one day on the way to school, a big dog was barking and coming toward us. I picked up a stick and approached the dog. I moved the stick back and forth and told the dog to go away. To my surprise, the dog went away. I very was proud of myself that day. To me, it seemed I had possibly saved my brothers' and sister's lives.

People were killed on a daily basis in Belle Glade due to drug violence. I did not know it at the time, but during the 1980s, crack cocaine and the AIDS epidemic were destroying Belle Glade. I remember cars with large antennas and fancy wheel rims. Loud music was played constantly.

The building we lived in always seemed to have something going on. There were gambling, prostitution, and drug activities at all times of the day and night. We began to get used to gunshots or police sirens every night. As long as everyone was in the house at night, we felt safe inside the apartment.

Mother was usually home before dark, but when she was not it was sometimes scary. It was a pleasure seeing her walk through the door every night. Knowing she was there was a comforting feeling.

The violence increased, and at least two or three people were killed every night. Women were raped at a high rate. We would hear little girls screaming as they were being raped in the outside restroom, but there was nothing we could do to help. Mother was strict about her rule that we mind our own business. Women were also being raped as they walked home during the night. Belle Glade was not a safe place for a woman at night.

Mom began to worry more about our family safety. Mother advised us that no one was allowed to go outside alone for any reason. We were to take our baths before Mom arrived home from work. On rare occasions, Mother was the only person who ever left the house at night. The violence at the time made it difficult to concentrate on homework or get a good night's rest. As the violence continued, Mother devised another strategy to keep us safe. We were instructed that if we needed to use the restroom at night, I remember urinating in a bucket inside the house. I felt bad for my sisters for having to comply with Mom's newest rule.

Mother and my sister worked well together. They began to make all the family decisions together. But I did not agree with Marnelle dropping out of school. It made me feel bad.

We continued to attend church every Sunday, as Mom found it more comfortable in church. As the violence increased, we attended church more often and began to get more involved in church activities. Mother and Marnelle helped with fundraisers for the church. We also volunteered to clean the church and other church activities. Although we were going to church more frequently, Mother still had us home before dark.

We were told never to go to the "rich side" of Belle Glade after dark. We consider the "rich side" of Belle Glade with the larger home to be the "rich side" of Belle Glade.

The walk back and forth to church was fun. My siblings and I would play along the way and create imaginary games. We imagined owning different homes that we saw along the way. We owned the nice cars we saw parked or those that passed us along the way. The trips to church were fun because we were able to temporarily forget about where we lived, the horrible conditions we lived in, and our safety.

When the nuns and priests heard our story, they took turns walking us home. I was afraid for the nuns when they walked back to the church. I was mostly afraid for white nuns walking alone in a black community. The nuns showed no fear as they walked back to the church. The nuns saw this as an opportunity to help more families in similar circumstances, and they began to reach out to the black community.

The nuns' presence in the community prompted more kids to attend church. Soon, instead of being the only family from our apartment building attending the Catholic Church, several families began attending. Soon we began to see priest preaching and helping others in our community.

I could not believe that with all of the violence no one attacked the nuns or the priests as they moved in and out of the neighborhood. My mother felt good and was proud to be a part of the church.

Marnelle and Mother continued to work hard in the fields. You could not separate the two of them. If you saw my Mother, you knew Marnelle was not too far behind. Marnelle and Mother bonded so well with each other, and it was fun to watch them work together.

The church was unaware of our food situation and how we lived. Our financial situation did not seem to improve with Marnelle working in the fields. We continued to eat bread and sugar water, rarely having any hot meals at home. School continued to be our main source for hot meals. We would arrive at the school one hour early, waiting at the school cafeteria to eat. We were very hungry and wanted to be the first in line to eat.

One day when we returned home after school, to our surprise Marnelle and Mother were home. I thought something had happened because they were never home that early. They would usually arrive from the bean fields just before dark. Mother called a family meeting. She explained that life was not going to always be easy or fair. She further explained that we would always have to work harder and should never give up on our dreams. She further explained that she knew our food situation was not improving, but she had a plan. Mother did not share her plan with us at that the time.

To our surprise, she told us that were moving to another building. The move was scheduled to be done over the weekend. I was excited about the move to the new apartment, but I wondered why we were moving to another apartment when we needed food. I missed the hot meals, and I did not enjoy being hungry at night. Then I thought about all of the shooting and how close the violence was to our apartment. Even though I did not know my mother's plans, I knew that I would not miss this apartment.

Saturday morning we began to move. Mother had some guys in a pickup truck come to move our beds and other furniture to the new apartment. We did not have much to move at the time. It only took two or three truck loads to move all of our belongings to the new apartment. The new third-floor apartment had a living room, kitchen, bathroom and one bedroom. There was no central air or heat. There was only three entrance into apartment. Overall, I liked the apartment. That afternoon, Mother explained that all of her rules still applied, and we were to strictly adhere to the rules.

The relocation to the new apartment was a smart move by mother. She moved the family away from the violence. Violence was no longer at our front door. There was no need to walk outside to use the restroom or cook hot meals on dirty plywood. Mother made the sacrifice necessary for the family to move to a safer environment.

The shootings and killings continued. The police sirens were not as close as they had been in the other first-floor apartment. Hearing girls being raped in the restrooms was a distant memory. The sacrifice that Mother made to change the family's living condition was a power move. She gave up hot meals for her children, additional clothing, furniture for the house, and other "luxuries" to ensure our safety.

Chapter 3
New Beginning

We were surrounded by fieldworkers and Haitians at the new apartment. We were treated differently at the new apartment building by the residents. Mother knew some of the neighbors from Haiti; she also knew some of the family members that lived in the building.

There are Haitian traditions that Haitians honored even in America. If you grew up in a Haitian community back in Haiti and were good friends or respected in the community back in Haiti, then you would be treated the same in the United States as if you were back in Haiti.

When some of the individuals began to find out about mother's past, things changed for our family. They kept an extra eye out for us when my mother was not around or was working out in the fields. At the time, Mother did not allow us to open the door for anyone. So some of the neighbors would speak to us through the door to make sure that we were behaving, had done our homework, or we had completed our chores before Mom came home. It was as if we were living in a community that cared about all of the values that my mother was teaching her children. After a few months, Mother loosened one of her rules. She allowed us to go outside on the third floor, only to play with the other kids. We did not have any toys. We would either play with the other kids' toys or play imaginary games that did not require any toys.

Although we had moved to a new apartment, we were not eating daily hot meals. We continued to have bread and sugar water. Mother never gave up on her principles. We were not to take food from the neighbors–or anyone, for that matter.

Marnelle and Mom were working six days a week. Their days began around four thirty in the morning, and they would arrive home between six and seven at night. They never complained that they were working hard or that they were tired. The hard work continued every day.

Mother was pregnant at the time; none of us knew it. Although I think Marnelle knew she was pregnant, she did not reveal it to anyone. I think Mother worked harder during her pregnancy. She continued to do everything as if she were not pregnant. During her pregnancy, I began to notice my mother talking to a man outside the house. She never introduced him to any of us. Sometimes they would talk for hours before Mother would come inside the house to prepare us for the next day.

The conversations continued for a long time, and we all wanted to know who the man was she was spending so much time talking to at night in front of the house. Whoever this guy was, made her happy. When my mother came in after having conversations with him, we could tell that she was enjoying his company.

As she approached the end of her pregnancy, her stomach was larger and more noticeable. She called a family meeting to inform us that she was going away for a little while. She told us that Marnelle was in charge and that anything Marnelle said for us to do was the law. We were to listen to Marnelle as if she was Mother and not give Marnelle any problems.

Mother was admitted into the hospital the following week. During mother's short stay in the hospital, the man my mother was spending a lot of time speaking to at night checked on us every day. He never asked us to open the door. After speaking to us through the door, he would sit outside the door as if he was protecting us. On one occasion he and some of his friends played dominos near our apartment. He let us know that he was close by if we needed him.

After a short stay in the hospital, Mother returned home with a small baby girl. She named her Wendy. Mother appeared to be in some pain, but she did not complain. Mother picked up right where she left off before going to the hospital.

One Saturday morning, the man our mother never introduced us to came by the house. Mother sat us all down and explained to us that the man that she had been speaking to name was Russell Alphonse. She explained to us that he was going to take us on a short trip to purchase some food at the flea market. All of us got excited, because we knew that we would have hot meals. What we did not know was the trip meant a one-and-a-half-hour drive to Miami. All of us got into a four-door Buick and began on our journey. I enjoyed the long ride. We had not been out of Belle Glade since our arrival. It was fun watching buildings and different cars along the way. I really enjoyed watching the electrical lines. The poles looked like they were Transformers, as in the cartoon. I love the way that the poles were designed.

When we finally arrived in Miami the "transformers" were gone, and we were back to the regular poles with streetlights. Russell pulled into the flea market and parked. Mother gave us strict instructions to stay together and not to leave her side. We were surrounded by food and other vendors. There was a lot of noise from all of the transactions that were taking place. I understood why she asked us to stay close.

I enjoyed how Russell took control of some decisions. Mother had not fully recovered and was having difficulties. I was guessing that mother was concerned with the final bill. I was thinking about how many hot meals we were going to have for the week or month. Russell continued to shop as if money was not an issue. He told my mother to get more food. He began to become concerned that all of the food would not fit in the car. When he suggested that we stop shopping, my mother agreed. The checkout line seemed like an hour wait. We waited patiently, and when we finally reached the cashier, Mother reached in her purse to pay for the all of the food that was purchased. Russell would not allow her to pay for anything. He reached in his pocket and paid the entire bill himself. When we got back to the car, I was wondering how the food was going to fit into the car. I watched Russell strategically place the bags in the trunk of the car. When he ran out of space in the trunk, he used the rear dashboard and the floorboard so everything fit.

We were on our way back to Belle Glade. Russell managed getting everyone safely in the vehicle. As the vehicle accelerated, I began to daydream, wondering how long it would take to return to Belle Glade. I wondered what would happen if Russell lived with us. It was obvious that my mother liked him, and although none of my siblings knew him personally, we'd immediately felt respect for him. Most importantly, we liked him too. He did not say much, but his actions spoke loudly.

I began to think about my dad back in New York. Something inside of me was missing my dad. I began to question what was wrong with him. Why would he let Mother leave? Why were our lives this way? Did he love us? Would he care for his children? Although I was happy for Mother that she'd found someone she enjoyed, I kept wondering what went wrong. I did not realize it, but I daydreamed so much that the next thing I knew we were in front of the apartment building. Russell took the lead and began to carrying items up the stairs. We immediately followed. One by one, we carried the groceries up to the apartment as night fell. Suddenly, gunshots broke out. Everyone entered the apartment and locked the door. I could hear the police sirens as they got closer to the building. We were not as scared with Russell in the house. Wendy was in my mother's arms; Steve and I were in Russell's arms. The police were walking the floors looking for suspects. Russell stayed with us that night.

I woke to a happy mother and the smell of eggs. She cooked eggs with onions on fresh bread; the orange juice was nice and cold. As I enjoyed breakfast with a smile, I wondered if we would be this happy if my father were around. Mother took some meat out of the freezer and placed it in the sink. I knew we were going to have a hot dinner.

My brothers and sisters were wondering if Russell would return that evening. He returned that afternoon with more drinks and candy. Mother prepared dinner, and we all gathered and ate dinner.

The following day when we arrived home, there was a bed and wooden TV in the living room. In the back room there was another bed next to the bed that three of us slept on. Russell had done it again. We began to see Russell more and more. He spent the night a few times a week. He was a hard worker and toiled for long hours. I remember asking him where he worked. He told me that he drove trucks for a living. He explained that sometimes he had to drive trucks back and forth to Miami. When Russell came home from work, I would take off his boots. As I removed his boots, I could smell the fields. We began to get used to having Russell around the house.

Mother called another family meeting. This time Russell was in attendance. Mother told us that Russell would be living with us, and we were to respect him. She also informed us that she was returning to work. Newborn Wendy would be attending daycare on the third floor, a few doors down from our apartment. Things were slowly turning around for our family, and we were grateful.

Chapter 4
Lifelong Commitment

Mother rearranged the bedrooms and divided one room into two rooms with shower curtains. Marnelle slept with the younger sister on one bed. The boys slept on the bunk beds in the makeshift bedroom created by Mother.

Russell was working all the time. Sometimes he would have to drive sugar cane to different parts of the state, which required him to stay overnight. It was nice having a man in the house, though having Russell in the house did not change our poverty status. We were able to have more hot meals, mostly rice with a little meat. We continued to be creative at times. We would make rice and peanut butter, jelly sandwiches.

The following day Mother announced that they had gotten married. Mom showed us her ring. She was very happy. We were also told that two of our stepbrothers and a niece from Haiti would be coming to live with us. We were all excited. We could not wait for their arrival. A few months later, mother and Russell went to Haiti to bring my stepbrothers and the niece home. While they were gone, Marnelle ran a strict ship. She made us do our homework; complete our chores, eat, and shower. Marnelle was stricter than my mother when she was in charge. However, all of us knew not to disobey Marnelle, because none of us wanted to have to deal with Mother.

They returned from their trip from Haiti with my stepbrothers and my niece. My stepbrothers' names were Rousselet and Willard. My niece's name was Farah. We did not have enough bed space to accommodate the additional family. Rousselet and Willard had to sleep on the floor. We begin to teach each other; we taught them how to speak English, and they taught us how to speak Creole. The boys decided to take turns sleeping on the floor.

We worked hard at teaching them the English language, reading, and math. As time progressed we begin to see some level of success with the English language. Six months later Farah, Willard, and Rousselet had picked up English. Within a year, I would say they had made more progress than most of the adults living in our apartment building.

The family continued to attend church on Sundays, and my brothers and I began to play more active roles as altar boys. Mass was at 3:30 p.m. There were only two altar boy robes, so my brothers and I would fight to get to church early, trying to be one of the two altar boys for mass. We would do our chores early on Sunday. We would eat early or iron our clothes early, just to be one of the altar boys for Sunday mass. We would even go as far as to begin to walk two to three hours early to be one of the two altar boys. One Sunday I got to church three hours early to make sure that I was one of the altar boys. I had no idea that the *Palm Beach Post* would be doing a story on the church. As we were walking out of church after Sunday mass, I heard the camera clicking, and lights flashed constantly. One of those pictures ended up on the front page of the *Palm Beach Post* the next day. I was so proud that I was in the newspaper. I felt as if I was a star after being in the paper. The competition was never the same after that day. I lost out on being the altar boy on a lot of Sundays. We felt even more special on the Sundays that Russell attended church with the family.

My mother sometimes allowed us to spend the weekends with some of the nuns or priests. I loved the time that we spent with the nuns the most. We worked at the church, pulling weeds from their gardens and mowing the lawns. The nuns were some tough ladies; they worked as hard as men. I admired the nuns' hard work, dedication and their commitment to the church. They taught us how to read and how to pronounce words correctly. The nuns taught us things from a different point of view. When we played word games, one of the nuns would teach us strategies and demanded that we not only pronounce the word correctly, we had to spell it as well.

When we spent the night with the priests, we would talk about life. The priests allowed us to ask them different questions. We would ask them questions about girls, questions about why God made people poor, or why people had to go hungry. The priests would always respond by telling us that God knew what he was doing when he created man and that God would always make a way. The most important thing that the priests taught us was to continue to have faith in God and to never give up.

I would question God about why he would take my mother though all of this pain and suffering, why she had to work in the fields as hard as a man, or why we had to go through many nights without a hot meal, but I also thanked God for bringing Russell in our lives.

The addition of Wendy, my stepbrothers, and Farah made a great impact on family finances. We only had hot meals with meat maybe two weeks out of the month. It was back to rice and peanut butter and jelly sandwiches with sugar water. I thought my brothers and niece would have issues with our living conditions or status as a family. They shared stories of their living conditions in Haiti. They had to go outside to use the bathroom, and they had to walk a block to use the hot shower. We were able to flush the toilet when we used the restroom; in Haiti they could not. Once someone used the toilet, they simply closed the lid. Each time someone opened the lid, the nasty smell would fill the room, making it difficult to breathe. I began to realize that it was not good to complain about your situation. When you think that you have it bad, other people have it worse.

The kids at school picked on us for being Haitian, for wearing the same clothes or shoes to school, and for our bald heads. We would discuss what we were experiencing at school with each other but not our parents. One day while talking about our experiences, I came up with the idea that we would swap shirts and pants, in an effort to make it appear that we were not wearing the same clothes every day. The only problem with that idea was that Rousselet could not fit into any of our clothes because he was much taller. He agreed that we should swap, although he was not able to participate. I admired the courage of his decision. It only took a couple of weeks for the kids at the school to figure out what we were doing. Then they began to pick on us for swapping clothes. Some of our clothing did not fit as well as others because of our sizes.

Mother always instructed us to immediately remove our school clothes. Mother always taught us to take care of our belongings.

Chapter 5

The Beginning

As our family began to settle in Belle Glade, Mother began to allow us to spend the weekends with the nuns and the priests from the church. We spent alternate weekends with the nuns and the priest.

The following week we decided that we would spend the night with the priest. He picked us up from the house, and we went to the church. We worked at the church all day. When night began to fall, we left the church and went to the priest's apartment. The apartment had a large room, with the kitchen on left side of the room and the living room on the right. There were two bedrooms, with a bathroom in between the bedrooms. We gathered in the kitchen and helped the priest prepare dinner. Once dinner was cooked, we sat in the living room and ate. The priest asked each of us to shower and prepare for a bedtime story. When it was my turn to take a shower, I began having a bad feeling. No one had done anything to make me feel this way, but I could not shake the feeling. As the hot water ran over my skin, I began to daydream. Suddenly, I heard a hard knock on the door. My brother was complaining that I was staying in the shower too long.

Once all of us had showered, the priest read us a book. I could not escape the feeling that something was wrong. The feeling would not go away. The priest was looking out the window and laughing. We rushed to the window to see what was so funny. When I approached the window, I saw a vehicle with black-tinted windows rocking from side to side. As I watched my brother laugh, something kept bothering me. I could not shake the feeling that something was wrong. One of my brothers asked what we thought was going on inside the vehicle. We continued to watch for a while, and finally one of my brothers said, "Let's go to sleep."

Instead of sleeping in his bedroom, the priest decided to sleep on the floor in the living room with the boys. The lights were turned off, and everyone began falling asleep. The priest slept in the middle of us. I happened to be sleeping on one side of him.

Suddenly in the middle of the night, I felt something grab and squeeze my butt, and then I felt him pulling on my penis. I was in a deep sleep, and for a while I thought I was having a bad dream. I remember that I was surrounded by my brothers, so I felt protected. Then I felt his lips and his tongue in my mouth. My eyes opened, and my teeth clamped shut. When I gathered my senses, I saw the priest attempting to continue to stick his tongue in my mouth as if I liked it, and he continued to reach for my butt. I moved his hand and tried to push him off me. My brothers were asleep and had no idea what was going on.

I continued to fight and push the priest away. He was stronger than I was, and he continued trying to pull me closer to him. Finally, I got a chance to pull my lips away from his, and I made a loud sound that woke everyone. My brothers asked me what was wrong with me. I was embarrassed to tell them that the priest had kissed me, pulled on my penis and grabbing my butt. I jumped up and moved next to Rousselet. I did not sleep for the rest of the night. I stayed as close as I could to my brother. I felt violated. I could not believe what happened to me. I wanted to tell my brothers about the incident, but the shame of it would not allow me to tell any of them. I could not stand the possibility that I would be viewed as a homosexual.

I needed to be protect my brothers from the priest, so I watched him. Suddenly he opened his eyes and looked at me, as if he knew that I was looking at him. We both understood that he'd done something wrong, and our eyes locked. There was another feeling there as well. He looked worried, as if I was going to tell my brothers. He made another attempt to come toward me. I shook my brother's shoulder and awakened him again. Rousselet asked me what was wrong, and I replied that I was having another bad dream. From that moment the priest knew that I did not want him to touch me or even get close to me. I would not allow him to touch me anymore.

The night could never end as fast as I would have liked, but the sun eventually came up. All I wanted was to be out of his house, to escape this bad dream. When everyone woke up the next morning, I did not want to talk to anyone. I just wanted to go home. When I told Rousselet that I wanted to go home, he replied that it was Saturday. I told him that I did not care. I wanted to go home, and I planned to start walking. All the boys knew that if I went home by myself we all would be in trouble because Mother did not allow us to travel alone. Frustrated, Rousselet announced that we were all going home. He apologized to the priest for the inconvenience.

When we returned to the apartment my mother was puzzled about why we'd come home so early and asked if anything was wrong. We said nothing was wrong. Rousselet explained that I wanted to come back home. My mother sensed that something was wrong or that something had happened while we were at the priest's apartment. Mother pulled me to the side and asked me again if something was wrong or if something had happened. I assured my mother that nothing was wrong and that I was fine. Deep inside me I felt terrible about lying to my mother. I did not want anyone to look at me differently. I thought that if I told my mother what happened she would call the police. Everyone in the neighborhood and school would find out. Once the word got back to the kids in school, they would pick on me and call me gay. I could not stand the idea that I would be labeled a gay person. During the 1980s, the AIDS epidemic was devastating the town of Belle Glade. We always heard rumors that AIDS was being passed from the gay community. I could not be associated with that community. No one would ever know that a man had kissed me and squeezed my rear end. I decided that I would never tell mother or anyone else what had happened that night. I never returned to an apartment of a nun or priest again. I no longer wanted to go to church, but I continued to go to church with mother because we had no choice. When we went to church, I did my best to stay away from the priest who had tried to molest me. I positioned myself to avoid seeing him or speaking to him.

When I returned to school the following Monday, I had a chip on my shoulder. I was angry. I began acting out in class. After several warnings, I had to be disciplined by the teacher. When the bully began pushing me around in the hallway, I closed my eyes and took a big swing at him. My punch landed against his face. I jumped on top of him and continued to punch him. Finally, teachers arrived and pulled us apart. Both of us were suspended for two days. I knew when I got home I would be in big trouble.

When I arrived, Russell and Mom were waiting for me. Both of them talked to me, explaining that what I had done was wrong and that I had to be disciplined. Russell pulled his belt free from his waist and began to beat me. After that, I resented Russell. When he asked me to do something, I either didn't do it the way he asked me or did not do it at all. After a beating from Russell, I had welts all over my body. My mother made me wear long-sleeved shirts to school to hide the marks. Deep inside, I wanted to tell someone what the priest had done to me. I continued to wonder why the priest had chosen me as opposed to one of my brothers. I am not implying that I wanted one of my brothers to be molested. I just could not understand why I was chosen. I often wondered if he chose me because I looked gay. Or was it because I was the smallest?

My rebellion toward my stepfather continued for months. I began to skip school, walking the streets of Belle Glade during the day. I didn't think mother or stepfather would catch me skipping school. In the morning I would walk to school with my brothers. My brothers thought that I was heading to class, but I walked off campus and returned to school at the end of the day to return home with my brothers. I became tired of being picked on in class. I was tired of getting in trouble and taking beatings at home as a result.

On one occasion when I skipped school, I ran into a group of kids. I decided to tag along. We gathered in the backyard belonging to one of the kids. Someone pulled out something that looked like a cigarette and began smoking. It was passed around to each of the kids. I watched as they puffed on the cigarette. They all looked as if they had done it before. Finally, the cigarette made its way to me. I knew that smoking was not good for children. However, I felt pressured to at least to take a puff, so I took a puff, inhaling deeply. I began coughing, and then a big rush of emotion flooded my head. I could not comprehend what was happening around me. I coughed and tried to breathe. I began to come down from the rush, and I felt different than before I smoked. Before I realized that it was not a cigarette that I was smoking, I began to laugh at everything. Then I heard one of the kids say, "This weed is awesome." He said where he'd bought it. I realized then that I had just smoked a joint, and it felt good. Three hours later the weed had worn off, and it was time for me to get back to school. The kids asked me if I was coming back tomorrow. I replied that I would return the following day.

I continued skipping school to hang out with the guys for several weeks. One day upon my arrival home after school, everyone was there waiting. I'd never seen Marnelle, Mom, and Russell home so early. I knew something was wrong. I was called in to meet with Marnelle, Mom, and Russell. They knew that I had been skipping school and wanted to know why. I told them that I did not know why. My stepfather asked me why I disliked him and what he'd ever done to me but show me love. I told him that I did not have any bad feelings toward him. I knew what I was telling Russell was a lie. I wanted to explain that what had happened at the priest's apartment was having a negative effect on me and causing a strain in our relationship. I wanted to suggest that instead of trying to beat the truth out of me, why not sit down with me and try to understand what was going on inside my head, try and understand what I was going through. I wanted to tell him that I'd begun smoking weed. But I knew that if I told him the truth he would give me another beating.

Each time Russell delivered a beating; the lashings came with more force and left deep marks. I knew that I was going to get another beating because of skipping school, and I was trying to limit the damage. After I explained myself to them, Russell threw his hands in the air and walked out of the house. Mother began to cry. I knew that I had disappointed her. Marnelle continued to talk to me and wanted to know what was going on with me. She kept saying that the way I had been behaving was not like her little brother. She knew something was going on. Marnelle told me that they were not giving up on me and that they were there to help me. I did not receive a beating that night for skipping school. The next day when we arrived to school, Rousselet walked me to class. Steve checked to see that I was in class. Willard check in the afternoon to see if I made it to class.

The finances at home were becoming tough. The additions to the family made things extremely difficult. We were used to eating rice, peanut butter and jelly sandwiches. Russell was not happy with our current status. The struggles we were facing frustrated him. Russell and my mother began arguing. Out of the blue, Russell began hitting my mother in front of us. I knew I was the cause of the fights, but I couldn't believe that Russell was hitting my mother. It was the first time that he had ever put his hands on mother. Hearing mother cry and try to fight back was difficult. All of us began to cry and yell for Russell to stop. Eventually he stopped and walked out the house. Mother stopped crying and told all of us to begin to prepare for school and asked us if we had done all of our homework. I told her that I was almost finished with my homework and I would take a shower after I finished my homework. I told her that I would iron my clothes before going to bed too. Mother told us not to worry about her and to forget what we saw. I knew that I had to shape up and that I had to get my act together.

I began to bring my grades up and stayed in school. One afternoon after school as we were watching TV, Russell and Mother were arguing. Out of the blue, Russell began hitting Mom again. This time Mother fought back hard, and all of the boys jumped in. Rousselet was more aggressive and pushed Dad and threw him off balance. Russell picked up a broom and struck Rousselet on the back, breaking the broom. All of the boys immediately panicked and we all stopped. No one said anything for a minute or two; we just stared at each other. Mother took control of the situation and told us that this would never happen again. She explained that Russell would never put hand on her ever again either. We were instructed to eat, take showers, and go to bed. Reluctantly we followed Mother's instructions and eventually went to bed. Russell never put his hand on my mother again.

Chapter 6
Opportunities

As Mother requested, the following morning we acted as if we'd forgotten about the incident from the night before. I began to wonder how many individuals had passed away that night. I'd heard gunshots close to the apartment building, as well as faraway gunshots. It had become common that someone died in Belle Glade every day. We hoped each morning that the person who was gunned down was not a classmate or someone else we knew.

Although Mother came home before nightfall, she stayed up as long as she could every night to wait for Russell. She made sure that he had a hot meal, although on most occasions we ate the usual. Mother always found a way to make sure that Russell had rice and some meat. He worked hard to support us, and we all respected that.

I waited for Russell the following night. When he came home I made my way to him and gave him a hug. I asked him to let me take his shoes off. Russell let me take his boots off, gave me a hug, and requested that I go to sleep. I felt good that night. I was extremely happy that things had worked out for me and that I'd made them happy. I suddenly began to wonder if I'd ever have a chance to make my father happy. I began to wonder if my father thought about us or if he cared about the pain and suffering we were experiencing. I began to analyze my feelings for my father back in New York. The more we struggled, the more I thought of him and how things might have been different. I wondered if Mother was keeping him away from us. Was she not informing us about his calls or giving us the letters that he was writing to us? I realized that my mother would not be going through these struggles if he were providing for her and his children.

During Thanksgiving and Christmas holidays were tough for our family. The school staff delivered can foods and a turkey to our home. We were not allowed to go outside during the holidays. Mother did not allow us to go outside because we had no gifts or toys. We watched TV or played cards. We could not wait for school to reopen after the holidays.

My brothers and I walked into the apartment after school and found my mother and Marnelle surrounded by bags of food. There was bread, boxes of eggs, candy bars, gum, soda, lunch meat, and more. I thought Mom had hit the jackpot. Usually when Mom and Marnelle were home early, it was because something was wrong. I knew that I had done nothing wrong, and my brothers always stayed out of trouble.

Mother called a family meeting. She informed us that she and Marnelle decided to start a business selling food, snacks, and beverages in the fields. Mother advised us that we were to continue to eat as if that food was not in the house. We were not to eat any of the food that was purchased for the business. Mother made sure that each of us acknowledged that we understood her rule. Mother never shared her plans with us or gave us any reason for her decisions. She explained that the reason for the business was being started was to create a better life for us; we were to trust her decision. She explained that she knew we are struggling. In time we would begin to see things change for the better. She confessed during the meeting that she and Marnelle had little business experience. There would be plenty of mistakes along the way. Mother explained that we had to try to make a better life for ourselves. She wanted us to know that whatever we wanted in life, we could accomplish. Mother inspired the entire family during that meeting with her passion regarding the business. She sounded so convincing. She believed in her new business as if her life was at stake.

We watched Mom and Marnelle price each item. We learned how the items would be sold, packaged, separated, and carried. Mother figured out ways to keep the drinks cold and the sandwiches warm. Watching Mother and Marnelle work through the ins and outs of the business was fascinating. They would get up at three in the morning to begin cooking breakfast sandwiches. The sandwiches were served fresh and mother knew that fresh food was important to the success of the business. As the business slowly began to pick up, a new challenge for business appeared. They were running out of sandwiches and therefore losing additional sales. Mother decided to hire people to carry bags of additional breakfast and lunch sandwiches. The move paid off and presented new opportunities for the business. The business continued to run out of sandwiches, Mom and Marnelle then hired two additional employees to sell sandwiches in other parts of the fields.

Business continued to improve. I was not the only one paying close attention to the business. My brothers and sisters were equally impressed with the new business. We learned a lot about how to run a business. Watching them start a business from nothing and grow the business had a profound impact on the entire family.

One nice sunny day after school, I suggested that we walk to the bean field and help mother pick beans. In the beginning my brothers were hesitant and questioned whether it was a good idea. I convinced my brothers that if we were able to pick a few extra hampers per day, would help mother with bills. I further explained to my brothers that if we were able to pull it off and keep our grades up, mother would be able to cook more hot meals. Maybe we would be able to afford to purchase cable. We told no one of our plans. The following day after school we went to the bean field. When we arrived at the bean field, there were only about forty-five minutes left before the fields closed. Mother saw us, and began crying. I told her that it was my idea and that we were there to help her and Marnelle. I asked how much was required to be in each hamper. Mother gave us our instructions; we decided to work as a team. We filled one hamper at a time. Then we took off to pick beans. The first day we picked two hampers. Within two weeks' time we were picking four hampers a day. We continued our pattern of going to school, walking to the bean field after school, arriving home with Marnelle and Mom before dark. We completing our homework, and washing our school clothes.

One Sunday Mother called a family meeting and told us not to come back to the field. She explained that she never wanted us to work in the fields, that God had better things in store for us. She explained that the extra income we were bringing in from the field was a great help; however, allowing her kids to work in the fields was against her principles. She said working in the fields would not allow us the opportunity to become doctors, lawyers, airplane pilots, or a greater career. She also explained that if she could go back in time, she would not have let Marnelle drop out of high school to work in the fields. She told us that life was going to get better. We had to continue fighting and never give up on our dreams. She warned us not to step on other individuals to reach the top. She said, "Work because you love what you are doing, and choose the job that is going to make you happy." She emphasized that it was our duty to be successful. Mother further explained that the harder we worked, the easier life would become. Mother said that if we wanted to help her and get out of our current situation. We had to work hard, study, and go to school every day. Mother promised us that if we continued to work hard, we would be successful beyond our wildest dreams.

Mother talked about how we'd lived when we'd first moved to Belle Glade, how close we were to the violence in our first apartment, and the fact that we used the restroom and cooked outside the house. She told us that we were going to move to a different apartment, with a larger restroom and kitchen. Marnelle would be moving into her own apartment a few doors down. Mother wanted one of the boys to move in with Marnelle and asked which one of us would volunteer. None of the boys answered, so I raised my hand and told Mother that I would move in with Marnelle.

Although we were frustrated that Mother stopped us from working out in the fields, we realized that Mother knew what was best for us. She often told us that we could be great businessmen in charge of our own companies. She said we had the potential to be anything that we wanted to be in life. Mother continued to stress that good things always happened to hard-working people.

Since we could no longer go to the fields, I wanted to find another way that I could contribute to the house. I began thinking about what I could do to earn money, what type of business I could start. Each day on the way home from school, I looked for opportunities or ideas to create a business.

The sun glared into my eyes as I woke up. As I gathered my thoughts, Mother asked us to brush our teeth. After breakfast, Mother handed us money for haircuts. I knew that having a shining bald head was nothing but trouble for me at school. Off to the barbershop we went. As I walked by the peanut stand on my way to into the barbershop, I began thinking that I could sell peanuts in the afternoons after school. I knew that my mother would say no if I asked her, so I came up with a plan. I decided to ask the peanut man for a job selling peanuts to the surrounding business community.

I could not get the thought of selling peanuts out of my head. I made up my mind that I would approach the owner of the peanut stand and ask him for the job. As I walked home that day, I began to practice what I would say to the owner. Then I saw the owner preparing to open. I approached him. I said hello and told him my name was Hydn Rousseau. He responded that his name was Steve. I wasted no time and asked Mr. Steve if I could sell peanuts for him. Mr. Steve asked me what made me think that I could sell peanuts. Where did I live? I told him I lived one block from his peanut stand in Royal Building. Then I said, "I will sell more peanuts in the same amount of time it takes for you to wait for customers to come and purchase peanuts in front of the barbershop." The slim man in his late sixties or early seventies was puzzled by my response. He did not respond for a couple of minutes. We stared each other in the eye. Finally, Mr. Steve told me that I needed to ask my parents first and that he had confidence that I would be able to sell peanuts. I asked Mr. Steve if he give me a chance if I received my parent's permission. I promised Mr. Steve that if I did not sell at least ten bags of peanuts after school, before dark, he could fire me after the first day. Mr. Steve said to me, "Young man, you have a deal."

I waited eagerly for Mother to come home from work that afternoon. When Marnelle and Mother walked in, I explained what took place at the peanut stand and about my conversation with Mr. Steve. I asked Mother to give me a chance. I promised that if I did not have my chores completed, if I missed any days from school, if I did not keep my grades up, or if I misbehaved, she could take back the opportunity that she was giving to me to sell peanuts. I promised her that I would be in before dark. Mother told me that she had to sleep on it and would make a decision in the morning. I tossed and turned all night and made sure that I was up at three in the morning to be sure not to miss her so I could get an answer before she went to work.

I offered to help Marnelle and Mother. At the same time both of them asked why was I up so early. I didn't answer. I had a feeling they already knew why I was awake. Marnelle gestured to Mother and asked her to give me a chance. Mother said that she would allow me to sell peanuts, but the first time anything went wrong, I wouldn't be able sell peanuts anymore.

I was very happy when I went to school that day. I made sure not to upset anyone, student or staff. I made sure all of my assignments were complete, and I did most of my homework during lunch and in the down time in other classes. Nothing was going to stop me from selling peanuts. I was determined to make sure that I did not disappoint my mother.

After school, I made my way to the peanut stand. Mr. Steve was surprised to see me. He asked, "How can I help you?" as if the conversation that we'd had yesterday had not happened. I laughed and asked Mr. Steve how much I would be paid for selling each bag of peanuts. He replied that if I were to sell the plain peanuts for fifty cents and the boiled peanuts for seventy-five cents, I would receive two dollars for every twenty bags of plain peanuts I sold and three dollars for every twenty bags of boiled peanuts that I sold. I asked Mr. Steve to give me ten bags of each. He reluctantly did so and reminded me that I would be fired if I didn't. Mr. Steve placed the bags of peanuts into two large bags, and off I went.

As I walked, I thought about my sales pitch and which areas I would cover. I decided to walk to the police station, local business, and City Hall.

I walked into the police station and rang the doorbell; a police officer opened the door. I explained to the officer that it was my first day selling peanuts and if I did not sell ten bags of peanuts before dark I would be fired. The officer told me that he could not make any promises, but he would walk me around the station. I could ask if anyone wanted to purchase peanuts. As soon as I walked in, the officer reached into his pocket and pulled out a dollar bill and asked me how much for the boiled peanuts. I replied, "Seventy-five cents." The officer gave me the dollar and said to keep the change.

He walked me to each office in the station. By the time I left the station I had sold six bags of peanuts and earned an extra dollar in tips. I left the police station and headed east. There was a bar a couple of blocks down from the police station. I followed my instincts and walked inside. I heard someone say, "We are closed until six." In response I said, "My name is Hydn Rousseau, and I am selling peanuts." The woman told me not to enter the bar because I was underage. I looked at her and complimented her outfit. I told her that if I did not sell ten bags of peanut by the end of the day, I would lose my job. I looked at her as if my life depended on her buying my peanuts. She said, "Please don't look at me that way, because I am a sucker for kids." I continued to stand there staring into her eyes, and finally she asked the cost of the peanuts. She asked to purchase five bags and reached into her pocket to pay for the peanuts. She also gave me a dollar tip.

I continued on my mission and headed in the other direction on the opposite side of the main highway. I walked into an office called EF Hutton. No one was in the lobby. A short gentleman walked around the corner and saw me there. I told him that I was selling peanuts and that if I did not sell ten bags of peanuts I would be fired. The gentleman purchased four bags of peanuts and gave me a two-dollar tip.

I walked to each of the units and made my sales pitch, asking all of the customers if it was okay for me to return the next day. I sold out my peanuts in the business park. I returned to the peanut stand and gave Mr. Steve all of the money for the peanuts. Mr. Steve advised me that I would be paid on Friday. I told him that was not a problem. I had earned more money from tips than I did selling peanuts that day. I was extremely excited and couldn't wait to get home to tell my family.

Chapter 7

Take Advantage of Your Opportunities

I was excited when I got home and told my family about my first day of selling peanuts. Two weeks later, my brothers began selling peanuts after school as well.

I learned at an early age that relationships are important. I formed relationships with all of the police officers, many of the bankers, car salesmen, and EF Hutton. I did not know at the time that the gentleman I was selling peanuts to at EF Hutton was also the mayor of Belle Glade. I admired him from the first day I met him. There was a different feeling about the man. When I walked into EF Hutton, I felt important and proud, as if there was something in the atmosphere. The office was nicely decorated with wood panels and expensive wallpaper and furniture. The conference room was beautiful, with a big polished wood table with matching chairs. I asked Tom if it was possible to clean the office or take out the trash to make extra money. I no longer wanted to sell peanuts. I wanted to be a businessman who dressed in suits. I wanted someday to have an office as nice as his. Each time that I asked Tom to give me a job cleaning the office; he told me that the company already hired someone to clean the office. Tom continued to buy peanuts from me on a daily basis, always giving me a nice tip.

When I was out selling peanuts, I paid attention to everything going on around me. I noticed that if anyone wanted their shoes shined, there was only one place to go for shoe shining. The shoeshine shop was close to City Hall. The police officers, firemen, and businessmen would have to go there to get their shoes shined. So I came up with an idea. I wanted to go around and shine shoes at the police station, fire department, and business offices. I began to watch the guys in the shoeshine shop, shine shoes. I paid attention to how they applied the polish to the shoes and the process that followed. I loved how they popped the rags as they talked to the customers. They always spoke to the customers with respect and asked them positive things about their day. After a while, I figured that I had seen enough to begin my own shoe-shining business.

Before I could start a new business shining shoes, I needed a portable shoeshine box with a stand for the customers' feet. I also needed supplies and a place to store my supplies. One weekend I thought about how I could build the box. Where would I obtain the tools to build the box? I did not tell anyone what I was thinking, not even my brothers. All day in school I kept wondering how I could build the shoeshine box and get the supplies I needed to do it.

I was thinking of the new business a great deal during school. When the last bell rang, it was time for us to go home. I followed my regular routine and picked up my bags of peanuts. I began making the rounds to my customers. I finally made it to EF Hutton, and that's when an idea came to mind. I figured that I would ask Tom to build the shoeshine box for me.

I explained my idea about the shoe-shining business to Tom and asked him if he could help me by building the shoeshine box. To my surprise Tom said yes. He said that he would build the box over the weekend and purchase the supplies. I told him that I did not want him to build the box for free. I wanted to pay him for the box and supplies. He said that I would have plenty of time to repay him. He told me that he wanted me become successful with my endeavor.

When I went to see Tom the following week, as promised he had built the shoeshine box. He had also purchased all of the supplies necessary to start my new business. Tom made me promise to take good care of my new shoeshine box.

I began selling peanuts and shining shoes at the same time. In the beginning I did not do a good job at shining shoes, but the police officers told me they would allow me time to learn, giving me a chance to become good at shining shoes. It took me about a month before I began to see my reflection in the shoes. I started receiving compliments from the officers and salesmen. After I shined his shoes one day, Tom told me I was becoming a good shoe shiner. I was extremely proud His compliment meant the world to me. Tom had a lot confidence in me, and when he said positive things about what I was doing, it made me feel like a superhuman. His comments inspired me just as much as my parents. As time went by I kept getting better and faster at shoe shining.

It seemed as though my life couldn't be better. I was doing well in school, my brothers and I were making money selling peanuts and helping our parents with the bills, and the new shoe-shining business was going great. With the extra income, we were able to eat more hot meals.

Then one day, out of the blue, Mom called a family meeting. I was puzzled about why Mother would be calling a family meeting when things seemed to be going great. Usually she called a family meeting because I had done something wrong. I looked around the room. I did not like the look on Russell's face. He did not look to happy and kept staring at Mother as she began speaking. Finally, Mother informed us that we were moving to West Palm Beach, Florida. West Palm Beach was approximately forty five miles east of Belle Glade. We were informed that the move from Belle Glade to West Palm Beach would take place within a month. Mother told us that the move would a two-part move and not all of us would move at the same time. The first move involved everyone who lived in the apartment with Russell and Mom. The second move would be Marnelle and me. Mother explained that the finances did not allow everyone to move at once. She further explained that until she and Marnelle were able to find jobs in West Palm Beach, they would continue to working in the fields in Belle Glade. When Marnelle and I moved to West Palm Beach, Russell would continue to travel back and forth to work in Belle Glade.

I was very frustrated after finding out that we were moving. I had worked hard to build up my client base. I had two successful businesses, and I was doing well in school. I was happy to know that I would not have to move first, which gave me more time to continue working. I had begun to enjoy my life in Belle Glade. I felt good in the afternoons when I walked the streets of Belle Glade, selling peanuts and shining shoes.

The following month the first move happened. My brothers and sister moved to West Palm Beach. I missed walking to school with my brothers. Walking to school without them was not the same. Marnelle and I stuck to the same routines as when the family had been there. I was too embarrassed to tell anyone about my family moving to West Palm Beach.

The next month Mom came to pick us up in a yellow station wagon. I knew that I had no other choice. I was so upset at the time that I did not say anything to anyone during the ride to West Palm Beach. I finally broke my silence and asked my mother if we could stop by EF Hutton so that I could say good-bye to Tom. She said no, we did not have enough time to stop to see Tom. As the car began moving I looked out the rear window, and I began to crying. All of the people I had come to know and built relationships with had just gone down the tube. I kept wondering why Mother would move the family to West Palm Beach when things were getting better for us.

Then the vehicle turned into an apartment complex. I could see my brothers and sister running toward the vehicles, happy that we had arrived. We hugged each other as if we had never seen each other before. My sister and Farah cried as they hugged me. That night I braced myself for the gunshots, but there weren't any.

The next morning Mother went to sign me up for school, which was next door to the apartment complex where we were staying. I liked the new school, and I made some new friends on the first day. That evening I asked my brothers if they liked the new school. They all agreed that this school was different from the schools in Belle Glade. My brothers continued to explain their enjoyment of life in West Palm Beach as opposed to in Belle Glade. I asked them why we did not live on the third floor. Wasn't Mother worried about the gunshots and the violence? My brothers informed me that there was some violence, but not as much as in Belle Glade. People were not killed every night. There were no gunshots near the apartment, and girls were not being raped in bathrooms or the bushes. They told me that things were different, and they really liked it at the new apartment. Although there was not much violence, there was a lot of drug activity.

I kept wondering why we'd moved. Although it seemed as though we were doing well, and it looked like things were getting better for the family, Mother knew that Belle Glade was not the best place to raise her children. She wanted to give us the best opportunities for graduating from high school and going to college.

Chapter 8

Fresh Start

The move to West Palm Beach brought a lot of new changes. We had cleaner apartments. There were two bedrooms with a large living room, a kitchen, and a dining room. The transition from middle school was going well. I met a lot of new friends. I was not being bullied, and it felt good. After school felt weird because I had no peanuts to sell and no opportunity to shine shoes. The boys at the school either football or basketball, that was not acceptable to me. I enjoyed shining shoes or selling peanuts. I wanted to be a businessman. I was not interested in basketball or football. I had an itch to get into something else.

I began to watch the drug dealers conduct their activities at the apartment complex. I studied them and the customers who came by on a daily basis. I also paid close attention to the drug users who lived within the apartment complex. I was surprised at the number of people who lived in the apartment complex who used drugs. I began to wonder why every apartment building that Mother relocated us to since we left New York was within a high-crime area. It dawned on me that no matter where we moved, we would be surrounded by crime. I knew that Mother was doing the best she could. Russell was driving two hours back and forth to work to provide a better life for us.

I knew that my plan to sell drugs would not work if I did not earn good grades in school. I knew my parents did not deserve what I was planning. So I studied hard and kept my grades up. I joined the band and began to play the drums. I tried to keep my mind busy in an effort to stay away from selling drugs.

I met some new friends who lived in the apartment complex. Those guys were bad news and I knew it, but they were popular in school. The girls liked most of them, and the guys stayed away from them. The leader of the group liked me. I thought being around him was cool. I began smoking weed again, under peer pressure. Some of the guys in the group sold drugs, and a couple of them owned guns. I knew it was a bad idea that I kept this information from my brothers and sisters. If I saw any of my brothers and sisters, I drifted away from the group and met up with them later.

I kept my attention on two members of the group, Derrick and Jeff. Derrick's mother's name was Ms. Janet; she was a single parent of two and worked for AT&T. Derrick did not need to hang out with the group. His mother worked hard to support for him and his sister. His mother never brought a man home. I had a crush on his mother. We always joked with Derrick that his mother was an attractive lady and that someday I would be his stepdad. Derrick was a straight-A student. All of the girls were attracted to Derrick. He was known as a playboy in school, and he had charm.

But Derrick was a part-time drug dealer. He went to school and completed most of his homework before school was out, unless he had a project or an essay. During the afternoon hours and before nightfall, Derrick sold drugs. He had a steady stream of customers who knew his working hours and where to find him. Most of the guys competed by running out to the vehicles of known drug addicts. The guys running out to the cars were either dropouts or adults who did not have to worry about their parents. Derrick would tell his customers where to meet him the following day, and in the evening he would go home and pretend as if he had been playing with the other boys.

Jeff told his mother that he was hanging out at Derrick's. Both Jeff's and Derrick's mothers knew each other and trusted that their sons were hanging out together. Jeff was a year older than Derrick, and Derrick's mother expected that Jeff would keep Derrick out of trouble. Jeff had his own customers and told them to meet him at the same location as Derrick's. Derrick and Jeff did not compete against each other; instead they looked out for each other. When either of them had a customer to approach for a drug sale, the other watched out for their parents. What was surprising to me was that they were more afraid of their parents than the police. They looked out for the police as well, but their parents were the primary focus. Jeff's mother did not play the radio (she was strict), and he knew that if his mother found out what he was up to. She would have no understanding about him selling drugs.

Jeff was six foot four and knew how to dress well. He had a very heavy accent, as if he was from New York, and the girls loved him. Derrick and Jeff hid their extra earnings from their parents. The fancy shoes and clothes they purchased never entered their homes. They gave those clothes to their girlfriends or friends to hide away from their mothers. They had everything figured out. The only part I could not figure out was where they got the drugs.

Jeff and Derrick were pleasant and respectful guys. Whenever they encountered my mother, they greeted her as if she were their mother. Mother liked both of them and treated them as if they were her children. Mom was impressed with their grades and told me that I had met some good friends. Derrick and Jeff came over to our place and spent time with me and my brothers. Everyone in the house enjoyed their company. Mother began giving more freedom to hang out with Jeff and Derrick. I continued to study Jeff and Derrick's operation.

Jeff and I spotted a couple of nice-looking girls. I suggested that we approach the girls, and Jeff agreed. But Derrick entered a four-door vehicle from the passenger door and then told us to get in the vehicle. Jeff and I got in. The driver asked us to put on our seat belts. We took a ride down town to Third Street and Tamarin Avenue, and then we continued until we reached Rosemary Avenue. When we arrived in front of an apartment building, a gentleman was standing in front of the building. He instructed us where to park the vehicle behind the apartments. I was confused why he was instructing us where to park, but the driver followed the instruction given to him. We parked the car and walked down an alley. Suddenly a door opened, and we entered an apartment through the rear door. Each of us was frisked for weapons. After we were frisked, we entered another room. Then it finally hit me … We were in a crack house.

I watched Derrick and Jeff as they negotiated with the drug dealer. Once the price was negotiated, the drugs were placed on a scale and weighed. The dealer looked up at Derrick and Jeff for their approval of the weight of the drugs. He then placed the drugs in a plastic bag. Then Jeff exchanged money for drugs with the dealer. He gestured for us to exit the building. Derrick led the way through the rear door of the apartment.

During the ride back to the apartment complex, no one talked about the transaction. Jeff asked the driver to stop by a store a couple of blocks away from the apartment complex. There I watched Jeff purchase a large quantity of small size clear little bags. As we pulled into the apartment complex, Derrick paid the driver. Once we were inside Derrick house, Jeff unpackaged the crack cocaine. The crack cocaine was reducing down into square portions. Then Derrick bagged the rocks into the small clear plastic bags. Once all of the rocks were bagged, they counted the total.

Although Derrick's mother was at work, Derrick took no chances that his mother would not arrive home early. Each night Derrick went into the bathroom. He reached into his pocket and pulled out a screwdriver and unscrewed the screws from of the medicine cabinet. He then removed the medicine cabinet. He hide all of his money and product in the hole under Neath the cabinet. I asked him to let me look inside the hole. I saw a piece of wood screwed in place.

I began thinking about how I could purchase my own drugs. I devised a plan to obtain customers. I took the next trip to Third Street and Rosemary Avenue with ten dollars. I doubled that to twenty dollars. In a week I had over two hundred dollars. I began thinking that I could become rich selling drugs. I could not buy any clothes or shoes, because I knew that my mother would discover something wasn't right. So I hid the money and drugs from everyone.

I started to get popular with the girls in school. I was able to buy things for the girls and members of the gang. I felt empowered because I had my own money. I purchased clothes and shoes, telling my mother that Derrick had given me his some extra clothes and shoes. As time went on, I acquired more clothes and shoes. I managed to accumulate a thousand dollars from my drug activities. To keep up with supply and demand, I paid individuals with vehicles to take me to see the drug supplier. Things could not have been better for me. I had finally found a new business.

Derrick, Jeff, and I wanted to purchase gold chains. We figured that the chains would enhance our popularity in school. Two weeks later, we purchased chains and matching rings. We wore the jewelry during the day and hid the jewelry from our parents at night. It was as if we were living double life. None of us thought that we would ever be caught by the police; the thought never crossed our minds. We continued our illegal activities and built up our customers and lied to our parents.

Chapter 9

Consequences

I was enjoying my life and my new-found popularity among my peers in school. I saved two thousand dollars as my drug activities continued. I wanted to earn more money.

One day a new customer approached me. I had a bad feeling about him. I had no one there to look out for the police. Against my better judgment, I continued with the transaction. It turned out that I had just sold drugs to an undercover officer.

I was handcuffed and placed in the back of an unmarked black vehicle. Many thoughts ran through my mind. I began to worry about what mother and Russell were going to think of me. What would the community think of me? Was I going to prison? What would the police do to me? It was as if a blanket was pulled off of me, exposing my secrets about selling drugs.

All that time I was hiding the fact that I was selling drugs from my parents and siblings. Now the truth had to come out. I was embarrassed about the situation. I was scared of what was going to happen to me. I began to pray to God to help me. The whole time I was planning and saving the money earned from dealing drugs I did not once think about going to jail. I thought because I was a teenager the police would not take me to jail. Going to jail was definitely not part of the plan. When the word got out, what would my classmates think of me?

The unmarked vehicle pulled into the police station, and the officer opened the door. I left the vehicle and was escorted up the stairs into a room. I was fingerprinted. Pictures of me were taken. I was placed behind bars. Reality quickly set in. I was in big trouble. I asked the officer when I would have an opportunity to call my parents. The officer told me that it would be a few hours.

Mother was waiting in the lobby, trying to get an opportunity to see me, to no avail. When I was allowed to make a call, I called mother and cried throughout most of the call. I knew that I had let my parents down in the worst way. Mother encouraged me to keep my head up. God would help the family through this situation. After I hung up, the guard at the detention center escorted me to my room. Once I entered the room the officer locked the door. I sat down on the bed and begin to reflect on my actions. I fell asleep as I pondered.

The following day I appeared in front of a judge in a courtroom. The judge asked me if I'd had the opportunity to hire a lawyer. "No, sir," I replied. The judge placed my file on his desk and called the next case. The judge asked the police officer to escort me back to my seat. Moments later a lady sat next to me. She began to shuffle through a stack of folders. Suddenly she pulled out a file with my name on it. She informed me that the court had appointed her to be my attorney. Her job was to make sure that the court was fair to me. She informed me that the judge would be calling my name soon and that the judge was going to ask me how I would plead. She advised me to plead not guilty. She requested that the judge release me to my parents, pending the outcome of the case. While she continued to speak, the judge called my name.

Again, I was escorted by an officer to the podium. The judge asked me, "How do you plead?", and I replied, "Not guilty." The attorney asked the judge to release me to my parents, the judge granted her motion. I was escorted back to the area with the other inmates from the detention center. Later we returned to the detention center. I was asked to clean out my locker and to turn in all of the items that belong to the Detention Center. The detention center informed me that as soon as the release papers arrived from the judge's office I would be released. Two hours later, the detention center received the release document. Finally my name was called, and I was informed that I was being released.

I walked in the apartment door, and I began to cry when I hugged my sister. It felt good to be home. I could not wait to get back to school.

The following day I returned to school. I did not engage in any illegal activity. Everything was going along well.

I had to attend several court hearings. Six months later, I was sentenced to one year of in-house probation. I had got off with a slap on the wrist. All I had to do was stay out of trouble for one year and this case would be behind me. The following day at school I met up with Derrick and Jeff. They advised me that they had to hang low for a little while. That meant Derrick and Jeff would have to stop hanging out with me for a while. It seemed as if I were a bad influence on them.

My relationship with Jeff and Derrick was never the same. I had to find new friends. That afternoon as I was hanging around the apartment, bored out of my mind, a group of guys walked around the corner. All of the guys were focusing on the guy in the middle of the crowd. He was always well dressed, and ladies loved him. I watched how everyone catered to him. I wanted to be just like him. I promised myself that I would surpass his accomplishments.

I was awakened on Sunday morning by the smell of fresh eggs, sausage, and freshly baked bread. The sound of Mother's singing was wonderful to my ears. When we arrived at church, my eyes locked with the priest's that stuck his tongue in my mouth. I could not get out of my head that he squeezed my butt. I stared him in the eyes and I showed him no fear. I gave him a look that dared him to test my patience. He suddenly looked down and away. I begin thinking about my plans to become the largest drug distributor in Palm Beach County. I found myself praying to God for his help in my quest. I made up my mind that I wanted all of the drug dealers to purchase their drugs from me. I no longer wanted to have customers approach me. I would only deal with the dealers.

I begin looking for suppliers. Instead of purchasing drugs from street dealers, I began purchasing drugs from Haitian drug dealers. Most of the Haitian drug dealers were impressed with my style of business. They loved that I spent time with them after a transaction was completed. I was taking a chance by resuming illegal activities under probation. I managed to keep everything from the family. I isolated myself from everyone in an effort to stay under the radar. I figured not hanging out with anyone would help avoid attracting attention to myself. Being on probation was the main determining factor behind isolating.

In the middle of the night, I would sneak out of the house and sell drugs for a couple of hours. Then I would return to the house and go back to sleep. Soon I had saved up $17,000. My goal at the time was to purchase a kilo of cocaine. The cost was $36,000. The cocaine would then have to be transformed into crack cocaine. I had not figured out how I was going to find someone who could transform powdered cocaine into crack.

During the time I was hanging out with the dealers, I paid attention to whom they would purchase drugs from and how the transaction was conducted. During my purchases, I noticed that the dealer took my money and entered a car and then returned with the drugs. Once the transaction was completed, the supplier returned to the vehicle and drove away. Over the course of six months of studying suppliers, I concluded that there were four main suppliers. One of the suppliers would occasionally speak to me. I was waiting for the right moment to approach one of them, but not before I had the $36,000.

Until then, I decided I would continue my routine. So I called my dealer and advised him that I would see him the following day. During school, I could not stop thinking about the $36,000. After school, I went home and changed clothes. I placed the $17,000 I had accumulated in a brown paper bag and headed off to meet the dealer. When I arrived, to my surprise there was hardly anyone around. I was enraged because he knew how much money I would be carrying. I was fourteen years old, with $17,000 in my pocket.

As I waited for the dealer to arrive, I noticed that the supplier who spoke with me was sitting alone, feeding some pigeons with bread. I saw this as an opportunity to purchase from him instead of the dealer. I wasted no time. I approached him. As I got closer, he looked up, and we locked eyes. His eyes widened. I said hello in Creole and addressed him as if he was my father. He said hello and asked me how he could help me. I told him that I did not want to disrespect him. I requested permission to speak freely. He gave me permission to speak. I told him that I wanted to purchase a kilo. His eyebrows arched. I told him that I only had $17,000 in my pocket to give him now. I would give him the balance in two weeks. I further explained that I would need him to transform the cocaine into crack. Then I said that I wanted to give him the money now. He could instruct me about what to do. For a couple of minutes he sat there in silence. Then he said to me, "Do you understand what happens to people who lose my money or product?" I responded that I did not need to know because I was not that type of person. I explained that I would never lose any of his money or product. He looked me in the eyes for a moment. Then he said to give him the money. He gave me the address to his house. I was to meet him there in a couple of days. I was excited. After giving him the money, I walked off. When I got home, I began to wonder if I had done the right thing. What was I thinking? I'd given him all the money. I had no backup plan. The days were long, and at night I had nothing to do.

I arrived at his home on a third day. I checked the piece of paper to confirm that I had the correct address. I knocked on the door. A woman answer the door and I asked for Gene. Gene came to the door and asked me to come in. As I walked through the house, I saw kids running around upstairs. I kept following him into a room. He turned on the lights and asked me to have a seat on the couch. He gave me a package and asked me if I needed him to place the package on a scale. I said no. He gave me some advice. He told me there were one thousand grams in a kilo and suggested that I make sales of twenty-eight grams. Then he said that he'd heard that most of my competitors were selling twenty-eight grams for $1,800.

I told him that I did not have a scale to divide the large rock. He gave me razor blades, bags, and a scale. Then he said, "I have faith in you." He said he would see me in ten days before he escorted me to the rear door. He asked me to walk along the side of the house to the front, where I got in the car and told the driver to take me home. When I got home I immediately divided the kilo into thirty-six bags containing twenty-eight grams each. I decided to sell twenty-eight grams for $1,200. That night I began to spread the word. I made two sales the first night. The following day, I sold eight packages. On the third day, I sold out. When I arrived home after the last transaction, I placed the money in a shoe box. Tomorrow was the last day of school. I would be graduating to the tenth grade next year.

I woke up the following morning feeling alive. Mother yelled for us to hurry and reminded us that we were late for school. Just as I approached the school steps, Derrick and Jeff grabbed me. They ask me how I was doing and if I wanted to hang out with them that afternoon. I behaved as if their asking me to lay low had never occurred. I said yes. As the day continued, I was thinking that I had exceeded Gene's demand for payment in ten days. I could not wait to meet with Gene that afternoon. During my last class period, my mind wandered in excitement. But I knew it would only be a matter of time before my brothers found out. The bell rang, and everyone began speaking loudly and exiting the school buildings.

When I arrived home, I placed all of the money in a bag. I gave the driver instructions about where I wanted him to take me. I always requested the driver to park the vehicle several blocks away from Gene's house. I did not trust anyone to know where I was going and did not reveal the location of Gene's home, which might subject him to home invasions. Gene had made it very clear that no one was ever invited to his home.

As I prepared to knock on the door, I was thinking about what I was going to say to Gene. The door opened, and Gene asked me to come into the house. He was home alone, watching TV. He motioned for me to have a seat. "What brings you here?" Gene asked. He flipped channels back and forth during the commercials. I informed him that I had his money, and I would need another package. Gene turned and looked at me. Thirty seconds went by, and my throat suddenly became dry. "Did you bring the money with you?" he asked. I told him there was $36,000 in the bag. Gene counted the money and placed all of the money back in the bag. He told me that I'd done well. I requested another kilo. Gene gestured to me to walk down the hallway to the back room. He turned on the lights and asked me to take a seat on the couch. Out of nowhere he handed me a kilo of crack cocaine. I told him that I did not like time-limit restrictions. He asked me why he should not request a time limit to return his money. I informed him that being under constant pressure made me feel uncomfortable and could lead to mistakes. Gene's face stiffened, and our eyes locked. Then Gene began to smile and agreed to the new terms.

As I instructed the driver to take me home, I was surprised at how easy it had been to change Gene's terms. I was also surprised that Gene did not question the fact that I'd kept the profit from the purchase of the first kilo. As I was placing the last twenty-eight-gram bag in the bag, I remembered that I had a meeting scheduled with Derrick and Jeff.

Derrick and Jeff wasted no time and asked me if they could purchase drugs from me. I replied that I thought they wanted me to lay low. Jeff replied that I'd passed that test a long time ago; we needed to move on. I told them the cost of the packages. They both purchased two packages and offered to hang out with the girls. I accepted their offer. I was becoming popular with the girls, and I enjoyed hanging out with all of them. We would strategize about meeting places to have sex.

Jeff said that his parents were out of town and suggested that we all go back to his place. Derrick and his girl stayed downstairs. Jeff and I went upstairs to separate bedrooms. My date and I entered the room and begin kissing. Passions were high, and the temperature began to rise. As I removed her clothes, she asked me if I loved her. I replied, "Yes." We ended the night in ecstasy and lay there in pleasure. We talked about our dreams and goals. *Knock, knock, knock.* I heard Jeff at the door. I put on my shorts and walked out in the hallway. Jeff advised me that he and Derrick had switched girls. I was not fond of taking turns having sex with girls. I refused to participate and told Jeff that I was fine with the girl in the room. Jeff looked at me and smiled as he heard the girl making funny noises downstairs. I repeated, "No thank you" as I closed the door. After our hour of fun, it was time for us to return home. I laughed as I walked up the stairs. I told that girl that I loved her to get her to have sex with me again. But I was more attracted to her sister.

I changed my sale strategy during the summer. I only sold to the dealers at night. That Friday night when I arrived on the scene, fifteen dealers were waiting for me. I completely sold out in two hours. It was one in the morning, and I decided to go home. On my way home I spotted the older sister of the girl I'd slept with earlier that night. We locked eyes, and I approached her. After a few minute of conversation, she asked me to come in the house. I asked if her parents were home, and she told me they were asleep. I told her to go and get a blanket. When she came back with the blanket, I asked her wrap the blanket around the both of us. I would kneel and walk beside of her in case her parents come out of the bedroom.

While I was having sex with the older sister, the little sister watched. The older sister walked me out of the apartment, and I went home. The word was spreading that I was the man with low prices. The girls loved all of the drug dealers. I was enjoying it as well. All of my dreams were coming true. I had created a new business that was making a lot of money.

Gene was surprised to see me again so soon. I told him that everything was going well. I told him that there was $40,000 in the bag. I wanted two kilos. Gene questioned why I needed two kilos. I told him that I was selling out in two hours. Again, he gave me that look and stared my eyes. I was handed two kilos, and off I went.

My parents and Marnelle were gone for the weekend to a wedding. I finally confessed my illegal activities to my brothers. I showed them the money and the drugs. I figured that it was time to tell them because I was running out of room to hide all of the money. They were shocked and could not believe what they were seeing. It was midnight, and I told them that I had to go out to sell more drugs. People were waiting for me. They said they would look out for the police or any sign of danger. We left the apartment and headed to the scene. My brother asked me what I meant by "the scene." I told him that I had everyone meeting me at the rear apartments. There was only one way in and one way out of the apartment complex. In an effort to make it difficult for the police to arrest me or the customers, I had lookouts at the entrance. If we were alerted that the police were on the way, we would have enough time to enter our individual apartments. The police would not know which apartment we went into. So I'd decided to call the rear area of the apartment buildings "the scene."

When we arrived on the scene, fifty drug dealers were waiting. We managed to sell $56,000 in drugs that night. My brothers could not believe it. The following morning I headed off to deliver $51,000 to Gene. Gene was shocked to see me—and more shocked when I handed him his money. He began talking about our future. He saw us moving a lot of drugs. Then he told me that he was out of product for a couple of days. He advised me to return in three days.

When I arrived home, I noticed that something was wrong. The door was open. I opened the door wider and saw that the house had been broken into. My heart raced as I walked to my room. All the shoe boxes were on the floor. Someone had stolen all the drugs. All I had was the $5,000 in my pocket. I was determined to find the person or persons who stole my product. The perpetrator would pay for his actions.

My brothers walked in and asked what happened. I told them someone broke into the house and stole all the merchandise. I asked my brothers to help me clean up the house before my parents returned from the wedding trip. We all pitched in and cleaned the house. I paid someone to fix the door. After we had cleaned up, I went over to Derrick's house and told him what happened. Derrick told he knew who the perpetrator was. How did I want to handle the situation? I was confused about what Derrick meant. Then he handed me a gun and told me to follow him. As soon as we approached the front of the apartment complex, Derrick spotted the guys he said were the perps. Without thinking, I begin firing the gun. The guys began running in different directions. One of them attempted to enter an apartment that was not too far away from me. I followed him and continued firing the gun at him. I was getting close to the guy, but a little girl appeared as the weapon fired.

I immediately ran away from the scene. I ran west. As I ran, I was thinking where to discard the weapon. I approached a store. Next to the store was overgrown vegetation, and I decided to bury the gun in the vegetation. Then, I ran through vegetation. When I exited the vegetation, I saw a opening in the gate at the rear of the apartment complex. I ran home and washed my hands with bleach and took a shower. I changed clothes and began walking around the apartment as if nothing had happened. My brothers came running in with a bunch of questions. Was that me shooting at those guys? Before I could respond, three police officers approached me and begin speaking loudly.

The officer in the middle asked for Hydn Rousseau. As if being called to step forward, I stepped forward. I was then asked to turn around and place my hands on my head. Then another officer grabbed my hands off my head, one at a time, and placed me in handcuffs. I was taken from the apartment and placed in the back of a police car. This was my second time in the back of a police car in my life at the time. I was not as afraid this time. The officer entered the car and drove to the police station. The ride to the police was short. Eight minutes later, the officer pulled inside a building. I was asked to get out of the vehicle and then placed in a jail cell.

I sat there in the cell alone, thinking about what was going to happen to me. For some reason I was not afraid. My actions that night did not bother me at all. I was not concerned with charges or what my parents might think of my actions. I had achieved and earned street credibility. My name would spread throughout the black community. I would never have to worry whether any of the dealers who were purchasing drugs from me would not snitch to the police if they were arrested. In the drug game, you are classified as a snitch if you give any information to the police. The police would not be able to protect you in the black community. The penalty for being a snitch was death. If the police were to place the snitch in protective custody, the snitch's family would be at risk of being killed.

I had now earned a reputation as a bad boy on the streets. Being known as a bad boy discourages other thugs in the community rob me. Robbers in the dope game do not want bad boys hunting them on a daily basis. Robbers look for individuals who will not retaliate if they discover their identity of the robbers. There was a mutual understanding on the street to stay away from robbers. Most of the robbers in the neighborhood ended up in jail or killed.

My thoughts were interrupted by the clicking of the officer's keys on his hips. He called my name and asked me to place my hands behind my back and through the slot in the cell door. After I was handcuffed, the officer placed me in a small room, approximately ten by twelve feet, with a table and four chairs, two chairs on each side of the table. The walls were black, and the lights were dim. A man walked in the door and identified himself as a detective. He informed me that he wanted to ask me a few questions. I would be free to go back to my cell in a few minutes. The first question he asked me was why I had been shooting at the other guys. I told him that they had jumped on me at a party and I was returning the favor. The officer then asked if I knew the guys as he slide the pictures across the table. I did recognize two of the men pictured, but I would never snitch. If I was to give the police any information regarding anyone was a sin. If I was to ever found out that I was the snitch. The penalty would be death. Snitching is forbidden. I told the police that I did not know any of the guys in the pictures.

He then asked me where I'd gotten the gun and the location of the gun. I knew that I had to be careful with this question. I told the officer that I had purchased the gun from an addict last night. The gun was hidden near a light pole down the street from the apartment complex. I knew that the officer did not believe my response. The detective wrote the information down on a pad as I spoke. He continued writing after I'd finished speaking. Then he asked, "Do you have anything to add to my report?" I told him that the whole thing had started over a girl and then got out of hand. I further explained that if I were faced with the same situation again, I would never purchase the gun. He continued writing on his notepad. He thanked me for my cooperation and advised me that an officer was on the way to return me to my cell.

I was fingerprinted, photographed, and taken to the detention center. We entered the gates at the detention center, an officer searched the outside and undercarriage of the vehicle. Then the vehicle proceeded through the gates. The car drove inside a building, and the gates closed as soon as the vehicle entered the gate. I was asked to remove all of my clothing. I was searched and given an orange jumpsuit to wear. The officer gave me a pillow, sheets, flip-flops, and a blanket. Then I was escorted to an isolated cell, separate from the main compound holding the other juveniles. I made my bed and went to sleep.

I heard, "Mr. Rousseau, it's time to wake up. I will return for you in five minutes." I got up, made the bed, brushed my teeth, and cleaned my face. The officer returned and requested that I place my hands behind my back and place my hand through the door slot. When the officer opened the door, he bent down and shackled my feet. The length of the chain was about eighteen inches long with hand cuffs on each end of the chain. The officer escorted me to a waiting room. Once I was inside the waiting room, he removed the handcuffs and provided me with a bag and a small container of apple juice. A little while later, I was placed back in handcuffs and escorted to an unmarked van. As soon as I entered the van, two officers jumped inside the van with me. The passenger door closed, and the vehicle began to move. I could not see out of the van, nor was I able to tell which direction the van was moving. Finally, I heard voices outside the van asking the officer for his credentials. The van entered the gate as it opened. I was taken from the van and placed in a holding cell. Then I was taken inside a courtroom. I remembered the process from my first court experience. The judge again appointed me a lawyer. This time the lawyer was a short man. He advised me to plead not guilty. When my name was called, the judge asked me, "How do you plead?"

"Not guilty, your honor," I replied. My attorney then asked the judge to release me to my parents. Russell, Mother, and Marnelle sat behind me. None of the others were allowed to enter the courtroom. The judge denied his request. I was being charged with shooting into an occupied dwelling and possession of a gun. I heard my mother crying behind me. The officer asked me to stand and escorted me to my seat.

The following day I met with my attorney. He advised me to snitch on person that provided me with the gun. He continued to explaining the benefits and how he would be able to work out a plea deal. He also mentioned that I would have another court hearing in two weeks. He would try then to get the judge to grant me released to my parents. He asked me for my permission to work out a plea deal.

Later on that day my mother and Marnelle came back to visit me. We had a good visit. Not once did we talk about what had happened. My mother told me how much she missed me and that she could not wait for me to come home. I told my mother that everything would work itself out. Two weeks later I was back in the courtroom. My attorney had worked out a deal with the district attorney's office. I was to spend one year in a group home. I accepted the plea. The judge called my name. He asked me if anyone had promised me any favors, was I on any medication, and was there any reason he should not accept this plea agreement. "No, your honor," I replied. The judge accepted the plea agreement and sentenced me to one year in a group home in Bartow, Florida. I was to be transported to the facility within thirty days.

Those were the shortest thirty days in my life. It felt like I went to sleep one night and then woke up the next morning at the group home.

Chapter 10

Accepting Responsibility for Your Actions

The van pulled up in front of what looked like a large house. The officer opened the door of the van, and I stepped out. The officer removed the handcuffs and walked me into the building. We entered a hallway and walked into a lobby. The officer gave a large envelope to the woman behind the glass window. Moments later, a gentleman came out and told us that his name was Jerry. He asked us to follow him to his office. As we walked to his office, I noticed that none of the girls or boys in the group home was wearing jump suits. They all wore regular clothing. As I looked around the room, I occasionally locked eyes with others in the room.

We walked into Jerry's office. The office had a desk, with a computer on top of the desk. There were two chairs on one side of the desk and one on the other side. Jerry asked us to have a seat. He sat in his chair and turned on his computer. He opened the envelope and began typing information into the computer. Suddenly, a printer began printing. Jerry walked over to the printer, grabbed the stack of papers, and placed them on his desk. He signed a few pages and then handed the papers to the officer. Jerry and the officer shook hands, and the officer exited the room.

Jerry advised me that he was my counselor. If I had any questions, I was to come to him immediately. He told me that my parents had sent all of the required items. He gave me a stack of papers. "These are the rules of the group home." I was never to leave the property without being in the company of one of the staff members. He further explained that I would be given a couple of job assignments and that I would share a room with another resident. During the day, I was not allowed to be in my room. I was to follow the program rules. Orientation was in the morning. Jerry opened the desk drawer and pulled out a map of the facility. The facility was divided into four sections. The administration offices were on the right of the map. There was a small library and classrooms. A portion of the building was off-limits to the residents. In the middle of the facility was a main common area for residents to relax in, one TV hanging from a rack up on the wall. The kitchen was located to the right of the sitting area. On the left side of the map were the dormitory areas for the residents. One side of the dormitory was for the females and the other side of the building for the males. There were offices at the each end of the hallways for staff members. There were two separate laundry rooms. The counselor then pointed to the rear portion of the map: the basketball court, patio, and walking trail. He smiled and said, "The guys love to play football. Do you have any questions for me?"

"Is there anything I can do to be released early and not have to serve the entire year in the group home?"

"Yes," he replied. "We have a rating system that we used to determine the residents with good behavior. If residents maintain good behavior, they could possibly be released in approximately ten months. In some special circumstances, I have seen some of the residents be released in eight months. Do you have any more questions?"

"No," I replied.

"Follow me to your dorm." Jerry opened the door to a dormitory. "This dormitory is assigned you." He gave me a badge. The badge had my picture, name, dorm number, and resident's number. "The bed on the left side of the room is assigned to you." I saw a black bag and a pair of shoes on the bed. "Dinner will be served in an hour. I will be here until six o'clock today, if you have any more questions."

The room was twelve feet long by fourteen feet wide, with a bathroom. There was a full-size bed on each side of the room and a twelve-by-thirty-six-inch window. At the end of the beds was desk for each resident. Next to the desk were lockers, with lock pads. The floors in the room were carpeted, with tile floors in the bathroom. I approached the bed and immediately opened the black bag. Inside the bag were towels, blankets, toothbrushes, lotion, a hair brush, and clothing. Everything I could have imaged I would need was inside the bag.

"Dinner is now being served in the kitchen," a voice over the intercom announced. I proceeded to the kitchen. Sloppy Joe sandwiches, fries, ice cream, and beverages were being served. I watched a little TV after dinner. A voice over the intercom system requested we all report to our rooms for a head count. There was a head count ever four hours. As I walked to the room, I began thinking that eight months in this group home would not be that bad after all. Two staff members walked into the room and counted me and my roommate. Then the staff members left the room. My roommate said his name was John. John asked me if I needed anything. I told him that I had everything that I needed. "Hi, my name is Hydn, but I'd rather you call me Rousseau." I took a shower and went to bed for the evening.

I began planning my strategy for being released in eight months. I would stay away from everyone, and I would limit trips and outings while in the group home.

The next morning I woke up with a positive attitude. I went to orientation and focused on the speaker as if he were the only person in the room. There were opportunities for me to obtain my GED and learn leadership skills. The group home required us to attend Alcoholics Anonymous meetings.

I was given two jobs. During morning hours I was assigned a job in the kitchen as a cook's helper. I helped prepare and cook the daily menu. After each meal I was required to clean the kitchen, wipe the tables, and mop the floor in the mess hall. All of the commercial cooking equipment and stainless steel countertops had to be wiped down. The floors had to be swept and mopped. My working hours were from 5:00 a.m. to 10:00 a.m. Monday through Friday. We were required to attend school from ten thirty to two thirty in the afternoon and a group meeting from three to four. Twice a week, from seven to eight thirty in the evening, we attended AA meetings. I attended all of the meetings. Some kids played sick or began acting out to avoid attending the classes. I remembered from my conversation with Jerry that I should attend all of the classes in my quest to leave the group home in eight months or less. I studied the individuals in the room. Some cried or laughed after their testimonials. When it was my turn to speak, I politely declined and advised them that I had never taken a drink. I noticed that after all the members introduced themselves, they would follow with, "I am an alcoholic." They acknowledged the fact that they were alcoholic and accepting responsibility for their actions. I stayed away from all of the other residents. I was determined to stay out of trouble and be a model resident.

After the meetings, we were to immediately return to our rooms for head count. John and I sat on the beds, waiting for the staff members to enter the room. When the staff members entered the room, John and I immediately stood. Then the staff members walked out and closed the door. John asked me what my plans. I told him that I wanted to obtain my GED. I wanted to stay completely out of trouble. John pulled out a book and began to read.

"Counts clear, counts clear," the voice over the intercom announced. I went out in the hall and saw a short man, about five feet four inches tall. I approached the man and told him that my name was Hydn Rousseau. He said his name was Steve. "Why are you in here, young man?"

"I was shooting at some guys."

He locked eyes with me. I broke the eye contact with him and looked down at the ground. "Would you ever do it again," he asked.

"No, sir. No, sir."

"Then take advantage of what they have to offer here and go home to your family." The way that Steve spoke inspired me. I told him that I was going to be a model resident and thanked him for the inspiration. I returned to my room.

My alarm clock sounded off at four fifteen. I showered, brushed my teeth, and got dressed in my white uniform. I was given my morning instructions. I prepared and cleaned meat, washed dishes, made donuts, and cleaned the tables. I decided that each day during my working hours I would pull out one piece of the commercial equipment and give it a Hydn Rousseau cleaning. I felt that it was my responsibility to make sure that all of the equipment was completely clean and free of germs. Someone tapped me on my shoulders and said, "Time to go, kid." I looked up to see the head cook smiling.

"I just have to mop the area, and I will be on my way."

I attended school and completed my daily activities. As I lay in the bed wondering about my parents and siblings, I constantly reminded myself that I had to work and study hard. I was not planning to go back to school. I was losing too much money during school hours, so I had to obtain my GED. I was not looking to obtain my GED to further my education. I was obtaining it to satisfy my parents. I knew it would make them happy. The GED would also assist me in my quest for early release from the group home. I was determined to obtain my GED while I was there.

I continued to stop by Jerry's office on a daily basis. Each time that I walked in Jerry's office, he was cheerful. One day in his office, I began talking about all of the money that I had been making prior to the robbery and the shooting incident. Jerry's eyes lit up as I spoke of my drug activities. Every day Jerry and I had conversations about my activities on the streets. But one day something was not right when I walked into Jerry's office after I had been in the group home for three months. "Is something wrong," I asked?

He stared into my eyes. "No, kid." He began laughing. I felt that there was something that he wanted to say to me, and I wanted to know what he was about to tell me.

"Jerry, would it be okay if I closed the door?"

"Sure," he replied. I closed the door and sat in the chair.

"Jerry, what is wrong?"

"I am about to be evicted from my home. If I can't come up with $1,200 by Friday, I will be evicted."

I saw this as an opportunity to help Jerry. I did not know how I would get the money to him, and I did not want to get in trouble for helping Jerry. Without thinking, I said to Jerry, "I can get you the money."

Jerry stared at me the same way Gene had done in the past. "Don't play games with me, kid. Can you help?"

"Yes," I replied. "How can I get the money to you?"

Jerry said, "You could send the money by Western Union."

I told Jerry to give me the name of someone he could trust to send the money. I told him that I would have the money sent via Western Union to person by Thursday. Jerry pulled out a piece of napkin and wrote the name of the person to send it to. I told him not to worry and said that he would have the money. The voice over the intercom informed everyone to report to our daily group meeting.

As I sat there in the meeting, I thought about the promise that I had made to Jerry. The truth of the matter was I did not have the money. Nor did I know how I was going to come up with the money. Out of nowhere, an idea hit me. I would call Gene. I knew that I would have to come up with a plan prior to speaking with Gene. So, I decided to tell Gene that Jerry was going to help me get out to the group home four months early.

As I dialed Gene's phone number, I wondered what I would say to him. I was facing that question when Gene answered the call on the second ring and said, "Hello."

"Hi, Gene, this is Hydn. How are you doing?" There was a long silence on the phone. In the drug industry, it is customary not to call any of your suppliers when you are arrested, shoot or robbery someone in the community. I understood that I was not to call Gene from the group home. There was always the possibility that the group home staff was listening in on the phone call. I told Gene that I was in a group home. I apologized to him for not calling him sooner. I told him that I did not think that the phone was tapped and that I had laid low since the arrest. I told Gene that I had a one-year sentence for the shooting at the apartment complex. I further explained my relationship with Jerry. I told him that Jerry was my counselor, and he was working on an early release for me. Gene asked me how early I would be released. I told him that I could be released in four months. "How can I help you?" Just what I wanted to hear!

I told Gene that I needed $10,000. I told him to send $2,000 through Western Union. I then asked him if he was ready to write down the information, as if he had already agreed with my plans. I told Gene that the money had to be sent by Western Union by Thursday. I told Gene that I would call him in a couple of weeks. Gene told me to keep my head up and that he was glad that I'd called. "I will take care of your problem today." Gene said that he had to go and hung up. I was excited and full of energy. I had pulled it off. I'd asked Gene to send Jerry $2,000 instead of $1,200 because I wanted to impress Jerry. I wanted to show Jerry that I could deliver as promised.

The following day on my way to our daily group meeting, I stopped by Jerry's office. He was cheerful and asked me to come in. He asked me to close the door and lock it. He then reached behind his desk and handed me a plate of KFC chicken. I could not believe that I was having lunch with Jerry in his office. That broke all of the group home rules. "Hey, I received the money yesterday. You came through, kid. Wow. You pulled it off. I am not going to lose my house. I am going to get you out of here in eight months." I told him that if he got me out in seven months, I would give him another $2,000. He stopped eating. "You will do what?"

"I will give you an additional $2,000 if you get me out of here in seven months."

"Have you been in any trouble since your arrival?"

"No."

"Have you gone to all of the AA meetings and the meetings in the group home?"

"Yes," I replied.

"I will make you a deal," Jerry said. "After you have completed six months in the group home, I will get you a couple of weekend visits to your home and get you released in eight months. In the meantime, I will work on you being released in seven months. But you have to stay out of trouble. There cannot be one bad report. You are to pay me the $2,000 in either case." I agreed.

I left Jerry's office feeling complete. I had saved Jerry from being evicted and made a friend along the way. I was suddenly promoted to head of the residence to oversee all of the responsibilities of the other residents. I was responsible for walking through each room of the facility to confirm that the areas were clean. If there was an issue with any of the rooms, I was to advise the staff members.

The following day I was called into the office. No one enjoyed being called to the office. That usually meant you were in trouble or that someone had left an urgent message. I walked into the small room at the end of the boy's hallway. "Mr. Rousseau, I have a package for you." He grabbed a yellow envelope and handed it to me. The phone rang, and as he reached to answer the call, he looked up and asked me to leave the room. I wanted to know what was in the envelope. My heart began racing as I opened the envelope. It was a letter from the Board of Education informing me that I had met all of the required scores to earn my GED. I was excited! I'd passed the test. I could not wait to call my mother with the good news.

"Hello." I recognized my mother's voice.

"Hi, Mom."

"What did I do to deserve a call during the week? It has been a couple of month since you called home."

"I know, Mom. I've been kind of busy."

"Are you telling me that you are too busy to call home?"

"No, Mama. I've got some good news for you, Mama. I passed the GED test." I could hear my mother laugh and cry as she congratulated me. "I told you I would pass the test, Mom. I will mail it to you today. Mom, I may be coming home next month for five days. I do not have all of the information yet." Mother reminded me not to wait another month to call home.

Most of the others residents did not like the fact that I got along with the group home staff. I had a bad feeling as I walked out of my room to conduct my daily inspections. I stopped by Jerry's office to say good morning to him. Jerry asked me to come in and have a seat. I reminded Jerry that I was on my job detail. Jerry informed me that he had a plan for how to get me out of group home while I was home on furlough. He said that he'd submitted the report to his boss and was awaiting a response. I was going home on a furlough in two weeks.

"I need a favor, kid. I am in a jam."

"What can I do for you?"

"I need $1,000 now and the remaining balance once I have your early release approved."

"Jerry, I will give you the entire $2,000."

"What?"

"Give me a day or two, and the funds will be sent to you by Western Union."

Jerry asked me stay out of trouble and to return to work.

I decided to start my inspections in the kitchen and work my way back to the dorms. The kitchen was being cleaned as I walked in. I informed them that I would return in an hour. I walk out to the dining area to conduct the inspection. I cited the gentleman for not properly cleaning the floors; the tables were not clean, and some parts of the floor had been missed. Out of nowhere, he punched me in face. As he tried to pick me up, I slammed him to the ground. I pulled him to me and grab him tight. Both of us landed on the floor, with me on top. I grabbed him and would not let him go. I could not believe that I was in the middle of a fight. My strategy was not to return his punches and to protect myself. It seemed as if the staff members were unaware of the fight. Finally, staff members arrived on the scene and asked me to let him go. I refused to release him without him telling the staff that I had not hit him. I knew that being involved in a fight would ruin my chances for early release. He refused to say anything, and staff broke us up. We were placed in separate rooms during the investigation.

When a fight occurs in the group home, both participants are removed from the group home and place in the detention center. All I could think about was going home for my furlough and my early release. Two staff members walked in to get my side of the story. I explained my side and told them that I had not thrown a punch. I was left in the room for a couple of hours before Jerry walked through the door.

"Son, I thought I asked you not to get into any type of trouble."

"He hit me," I replied.

"Are you telling me that you did not throw any punches?"

"No," I replied.

"Let me speak to the investigators regarding their findings."

I stared out of the window and noticed two police vehicles in the parking area. Was I being taken to the detention center? The officers were now in the hallway. I could hear the police radio. One of the officers asked which holding cell the guy who started the fight was in. The officer looked down at the folder that was given to him. Then the police officer placed handcuffs on the gentleman in the other room. Then he was placed in a police vehicle.

Jerry walked in the room. "Had you thrown one punch, you would be going with him." He told me that other inmates corroborated my statement. Jerry told me to go to my room and stay out of trouble. As I walked to my room, I noticed the other inmates looking at me. When I walked into the room, my roommate asked me why I did not fight back. I told him that my job was to return home and that I did not come here to fight. "You will be looked at as a coward for the remainder of your stay in the group home."

"I do not have anything to prove to anyone. Do they remember why I am in the group home? No one else in the group home is here for shooting at anyone. I am not worrying about what they think. I want to go home."

The voice over the intercom requested that I report to Jerry's office. "You are going on furlough next Thursday for six days. I have not heard anything from my boss regarding the early release. As soon as I know anything, you will be the first I call."

I called my mother and told her that I was coming home for six days. The following week I was placed on a Greyhound bus heading to West Palm Beach. Everyone was happy to see me. My mother just held me for a couple of minutes. I had not seen my mother and siblings since the shooting. We all cried and laughed. It was nice to be home. During my furlough, I was required to call the group home four times a day. The group home would also randomly call to make sure that I was home. Mother took us to church that Sunday. During the morning sermon, I kept praying to God that he bless me with an early release.

Derrick and Jeff came over to visit me. While we were sitting on the porch, the group home called. I answered the phone. To my surprise, Jerry was on the phone. Jerry informed me that I was approved for early release. "You do not have to return to the group home." He advised me that my mother would have to appear at a court hearing in a couple of days. I told him that I did not think that there would be any problems. He informed me that I would receive a letter from the group home with all of the details.

Chapter 11

Truth

After I was released from the group home, one would have thought I would have learned my lesson. But I returned to the same neighborhood and hung out with the same old friends. Jeff and Derrick were still drug dealers. I had not learned from my past wrongdoings. During my time in the group home, I'd earned my GED and learned leadership skills. I should have furthered my education and leadership skills. Instead of doing something good for myself, I resorted back to selling drugs. It was the only thing I thought would give me the opportunity to escape living in poverty. One year later, I moved out of my parents' house and rented a two-bedroom apartment.

I changed my communicating strategy with the dealers. I used a beeper, a device that alerted me when someone wanted to reach me. The beeper would display a phone number. When a dealer wanted to make a drug purchase, the dealer sent me a beep. I would return the call and find out the quantity of they wanted purchase. I had the dealers to meet me at random locations to complete the transactions. I never chose the same location twice for any of the transactions. I did not want to take the chance of being robbed by one of the dealers and out of view of the police.

A couple of the dealers who'd grown up in the same neighborhood suggested to me that we take the show on the road to Georgia. Their names were Black and Meat. Black was about 240 pounds and six foot five inches tall. Meat was about 160 pounds and five foot eight inches tall. Black reminded me that we would double profits. Basically, a kilo of cocaine sold for $36,000 in West Palm Beach. With the connection Black had in Georgia, someone who he knew how to handle the drug deals while avoiding the cops. We would sell the same kilo to the dealers for $72,000. Black further explained that once we arrived in Georgia, his connection would deal with the dealers and I would have to touch anything. Black knew that I did not want to be implicated if one of the dealers were caught by the police.

I told Black and Meat that I would think about it. I later pitched the idea to Gene. Gene advised me against going to Georgia. I told Gene that I wanted to give it a shot. Gene advised me to be careful and to watch my back. Two weeks later, the three of us were heading to Georgia. We chose a four-door Buick with dark-tinted windows. I had the vehicle serviced and all of the lights checked. I did not want us to have to stop for anything once we got on the highway. Black wanted to leave early in the morning, and we decided we would leave at 1:00am in the morning. That night I had that funny feeling again. Something did not feel right about this trip. Finally, we were on the high way. Black decided to start driving.

As the vehicle moved forward, I fell in a deep sleep. Black woke us up. He said he was speeding, and he thought he'd just passed a police car. I jumped up and looked out of the rear window. I told them that I did not see any cars behind us. A few moments later, a police car appeared behind our vehicle. Then the police lights and sirens began to sound. As the officer asked us to step out of the vehicle, I knew we were going to jail. The police dog took no time finding the drugs. We were going to jail for a long time.

Chapter 12
Failure

Failure is a necessary part of life. Most of us are afraid to fail for various reasons. Some of us don't want to embarrass our parents or friends. Maybe we are afraid of what our coworkers or neighbors would think of us, afraid of losing your status, afraid of the *unknown*. How are we to obtain experience, let alone wisdom, if we never fail? I don't look for failure, and I don't factor failure into my decision-making process. I always try to think through my plans. I plan for things to work out in my favor, but when things don't go as planned, I adjust the plan. When a plan fails, it does not mean that we failed; it means that the plan failed.

It is our responsibility to take a look at why the plan failed and revise the plan. In most cases, we spend too much time thinking about why the plan failed. Some of us take it personally when we fail. *Don't.* Instead, spend your time addressing the solution to the problem. Go back to the drawing board and revise the plan. If the plan fails after a revision, revise the plan again. The first time we learn to ride a bike, we plan to get on the bike and ride it up and down the sidewalk the first time out. When we fall off the bike, the plan failed. We did not give up on learning how to ride a bike. We revised the plan and got back on the bike as quickly as we can. Determined to succeed, we learned how to ride the bicycle.

I knew that I had failed at following the instruction given to me by my parents, teachers, and close friends. My plan to earn money by selling drugs was the wrong plan. My poor decisions would change the course of my life forever. However, I refused to let things end on a bad note. I was determined to take advantage of the situation. I knew that I had to regain control of my life and revise the plan. I will not stop revising my plan until I win.

So I revised the plan immediately. I knew that I would have to acquire the will, desire, and courage to overcome my old habits. I would have to either change my surroundings or change my friends. I would have to let go of the fear of the unknown and push through the obstacles ahead. I would pull strength from my family's belief in me. Mother did not turn her back on me although I was in a jail again. The faith that my mother had in me made me feel like Superman. It was time for me to prove to my mother that all of her hard work for me would pay off in the end. I had to live up to my responsibility and begin to do my part. I needed to take responsibility for my actions and devise a plan to make me a better person.

This time the judge did not place me in a group home. I was given a nine-year sentence in federal prison.

Chapter 13
Revising My Life Plan

As soon as I stepped foot on Federal Prison soil, it all hit me. Life was not a game. Until that point, I'd thought life was a game. The prison guard wasted no time informing me who was in charge. After taking pictures and fingerprints, visiting the doctor and answering all of guard's questions, I was placed in handcuffs and placed in a six-foot wide by nine-foot long cell with another individual. There was show in the cell and the room was small. In the group home the rooms were double and there was a shower in the room.

The room had metal bunk beds, a metal sink and toilet combination, and a metal mirror. There was a small window, six inches wide and two feet long. The entry door had a slot that was used to handcuff the inmate when necessary. The same slot was used to pass food trays and other items into the inmate's cell. There was also a six-inch-by-two-foot window in the door that allowing the prison guards view to monitor the inmates. Inmates in the highly secure area of the prison called "the hole." I was placed in that section of the prison because there were no open rooms on the main prison campus. I was advised that I would be in this section for approximately one month. No one enjoyed being in the hole, this section of the prison discipline inmates for inappropriate behavior. Inmates placed in the hole are not allowed to take showers or make phone calls on a daily basis. Inmates in the hole are allowed to take showers twice a week and to make a phone call once a week.

In the beginning of my sentence I did not call or write anyone because I was too embarrassed. I was still in a state of shock. I was not in a group home, where I might have learned my lesson. Instead, I was sitting in a federal prison. I had a hard time adjusting to my current situation. I slept most of the day, as if I were in a bad dream, only to wake up in the same six-by-nine prison cell. I began falling into a mild depression. I started feeling sorry for myself and isolated myself from everyone. I rarely spoke to the prison guards or the inmates. I did not write or call my family.

I was moved from the hole to the special housing unit. The special housing unit housed the inmates that required protection from the main prison population. Some inmates were in the special housing unit because of their high profile, celebrity status, or because they were part of the witness protection program.

I was watching the news with other inmates. I did not know none the inmates in the special housing unit. Most of the inmates were watching the five o'clock news. Everyone was paying special attention to one clip on the news. The reporter was speaking of the high-profile federal drug case against Augusto "Willy" Falcon and Salvador "Sal" Magluta. The reporter focused in on the fact that witnesses in the case were being killed or having accidents deaths prior to trial. Then the reporter went live to the crime scene in Miami, where another witness had been shot to death that morning. I did not know it at the time, but that day I was actually sitting next to Willy and Sal. Willy Falcon and Sal Magluta were among the largest drug dealers in southeast Florida at the time. I began to wonder if the two drug lords would attempt a jailbreak or harm anyone in prison.

There were stories that Willy Falcon and Sal Magluta corrupted most prison guards they came in contact with. They would corrupt lawyers and bribe jurors. I saw one of them use a cell phone in his cell. Everyone knew to turn a blind eye to those types of activities. If an inmate was to speak out against Willy or Sal, the consequence could ultimately be your life.

Inmates at the time knew that Willy and Sal were having sexual encounters with prison guards and women during visits with their lawyers. No inmates or prison guards would speak against Willy or Sal for fear of their lives.

Finally, I was moved from the special housing unit and placed in the dorm on the prison campus. The prison cells were the same size throughout the prison. However, on the main campus the inmates had more freedom. Inmates were allowed movement prison ground during the day. You were able to go from one part of the prison to another to every hour.

All inmates were required to have a job. There were jobs in construction, prison maintenance, and Unicore. Inmates were allowed to perform their duties between eight in the morning and three thirty. Inmates who worked in Unicore were allowed additional work hours between five and nine in the evening.

The prison guards did a prisoner count five times a day. at 2:00 a.m., 5:00 a.m., 4:00 p.m., 10:00 p.m., and at midnight. Inmates were allowed to eat between 6:00 and 7:30 a.m., 11:30 a.m. and 12:30 p.m., and 4:30 and 5:30 p.m. from the cafeteria.

I was wondering when will the orientations going to begin, the instructor walk in the door. I begin learning about the job placement; I began to learn the dos and don'ts of the prison population. The prison store, known as the commissary, sold common items, such as shoes, soup, tuna, peanut butter, hygiene products, et cetera. Most of the food sold in the store could be cooked in boiling water.

The gym and library were available to inmates during their free time. The library did not have any computers but offered magazines and books that could be checked out. A section of the library provided current law books. Some of the inmates spent their time fighting their cases by learning the law.

The recreation yard included the gym, a large running track, and an open field that could be used to play football or softball. Each dorm held two hundred inmates. There were four showers, three televisions, and a multiuse table in an open area. Most of the tables were used to play cards or board games. There were not a lot of options in prison. There were no rehabilitation programs to prepare inmates for returning to society as productive citizens.

There are three types of inmates: those with life sentences and will die in prison system; inmates with twenty- to thirty-year sentences who would return to society in their fifties, sixties, and seventies, and the inmates sentenced to fifteen years or less.

Prison life reminded me of the streets. The currency in prison was postage stamps. Inmates purchased a book of postage stamps from the prison store for the current rate. However, the value of the book of stamps was five dollars on the prison campus. Some inmates used stamps to gamble, pay other inmates to help appeal their case, pay other inmates for sex, or pay inmates to iron or wash their prison uniforms.

I had really gotten myself in a big mess this time. After my prison orientation, I realized that I would have to make some choices as to which direction I wanted to take my life. I was no longer in total control of my life. I would have to choose a job that would pay me eleven cents an hour or a job in Unicore that paid me $1.25 an hour, with overtime at $2.00. The jobs in Unicore produced items that were sold in the private market. I did not want a job by which the prison system would profit from my labor. I decided that I would take a job as an electrician at eleven cents an hour. I could learn a trade that I could take with me upon my release from prison.

My first day on the job, I went out on a work order call with the electrical prison guard to one of the dorms on the prison campus. After we finished the work order and were on our way out of the dorm, notification was sent out over the guard's radio that the prison was on a temporary lockdown. When the prison is on lockdown status, no inmates were allowed to move from their current locations. If inmates were within their assigned dorms, inmates were locked down their cell. If inmates were in the recreation yard, they were not allowed to leave. The notification also informed the officers that they were not allowed to move on the prison campus; the officers were to remain in their current locations until further notice.

I asked the officer why the prison was on lockdown status. The officer told me that when Manuel Noriega was moving on the prison campus, no one else was allowed to move on campus. I'd had no idea that Manuel Noriega was a prisoner in this institution. He had his own prison cell within the prison. Manuel Noriega's personal prison cell included a library, bathroom, and recreation yard. When all of the prisoners were secured in their dorms at night, Manuel Noriega was allowed to walk in shackles on the prison grounds as part of his recreation. He did not have any contact with any other inmates. His cell required guards to enter through double doors. Both doors could not be opened at the same time. He was closely monitored twenty-four hours a day via video surveillance.

When I was finally approved for visitation, I got a chance to see my parents. Before my incarceration, I did not know my longtime girlfriend was pregnant. She was present at the visitation with my son, and I held him for the very first time.

The time went by fast, and soon it was time for inmates to return to our cells. After each visit an inmate went to a room and removed all of his clothing for a full body inspection: cough, lift each leg, bend over and spread his butt cheeks. I enjoyed visitation, until it was time to return to our cells.

A month after being placed in a dorm, an inmate was killed in the showers. We were placed on lockdown for a couple of days. Rumors had it that the inmate killed was a star witness in the trial of the aforementioned drug lords.

The reason for the extended lockdown was because the investigators could not locate the murder weapon. The Miami Dade Police was brought in on the investigation, and divers were sent into the retention pond to search for the murder weapon. Tension was high after the murder. Inmates were afraid for their lives as well.

I promised myself that I would never return to prison. I realized that prison life was a dangerous life, and there was no guarantee that I would walk out of prison alive if I got into any type of confrontation with another inmate. I learned very quickly that as long as I was not involved with the wrong crowd, gangs, gambling or sleeping with other inmates, my chances of leaving prison were high.

I always thought that when individuals were sent to prison, the prison system would reform the inmate and help him to become a productive citizen. What I experienced in prison was different from my expectations. Inmates were left to learn from each other. In most cases, the inmates taught each other how to commit new or different crimes, how to improve their criminal operations, or how to become a drugh kingpin.

Kingpins, or high-profile inmates, were convicted for selling drugs, usually receiving long prison sentences. They would handpick other inmates who would be released within five to ten years and teach them how to run drug operations. They would provide their contacts and resources to the inmate being released. Not only was this learning process used for incarcerated drug dealers, it was used to teach white-collar crime, bank robberies, and other criminal activities. These types of activities increased the inmate's chance of returning to the prison system as a repeat, or habitual, offender.

I did not want to learn how to commit new crimes. I wanted to *decrease* my chances of returning to the prison system. I also knew that I did not want to be an electrician for the rest of my life. However, I would use this trade as a stepping-stone after my release, to give me a fresh start. I requested that my prison foreman be given permission to call on me any time of the day or night for emergency calls. I worked hard during normal working hours, performing service calls. I asked my parents to sign me up for a college course to learn how to be an electrician. I worked during the day, learning as much as I possibly could, and studied at night.

Because of prison rules, the college could not send my learning materials directly to the prison. However, my parents could receive all of my college materials and then mail the course program to me. Upon completion of each section of my course, I would mail the material to my parents, and they would mail it to the college. Once I passed the college course, I continued reading other materials related to the electrical field.

The prison built a couple of buildings on the prison grounds, and I was a part of the construction team. I had a chance to apply the knowledge I'd acquired from my college courses.

While I was working on the new buildings, the chaplain came to the jobsite and informed me that my mother had called. It was urgent that I call home. When I called, my mother informed me that my biological father had passed away. Although it was a shock to me, I did not cry. It hurt me that I would not ever get a chance to talk to him or get to know him. I wanted to have a relationship with him, and at that moment I realized that I would never get that chance.

I began to work as much as I could to get over my pain. I was happy to have worked to keep my mind occupied.

The buildings took two years to complete. I gained a lot of experience. Due to good behavior, I was sent from a medium-security prison to a low-security prison at Eglin Air Force Base.

When I arrived at Eglin Air Force Base prison camp, I was surprised. There were no prison cells or fences. The inmates had boundaries they were not allowed to go beyond. If an inmate was caught outside the boundaries, he would be sent back to prison. All of the rules that applied in prison applied at the prison camp. However, I was unable to obtain a job at the prison camp as an electrician. I applied for a job as a diesel mechanic, assisting the air force personnel, and I was hired. The prison camp's purpose was to supplement the base's maintenance operation. I quickly familiarized myself with the rules and regulations of the camp. The visitation rules were different as well. The inmates were not strip searched at the end of visits. The inmates were required to empty their pockets, and an officer would perform a pat-down search on each prisoner.

As my prison sentence came to an end, I appreciated being placed in a prison camp and was looking forward to being released. The prison counselor informed me during my release preparation that I was eligible to enter a halfway house for three months as a part of my release. The halfway house was a facility located within the county in which the released prisoner resided, designed to assist in the transition from prison to society. I took the opportunity to enter the halfway house. And I got a job as an electrician.

After my second week at the halfway house, I was allowed to stay at my mother's home during the weekends. During my weekend visits, the halfway house would randomly call the house to confirm that I was home. I was not allowed to leave without prior authorization. A month later, the halfway house allowed me to go home Monday through Thursday from five to eight in the evening.

My transition from prison to society was difficult. I did not know how to use a pay phone or cell phone. I did not understand the bus routes, et cetera. It seemed as if the world was moving at a fast pace, and I was moving slowly.

Finally, my halfway house tenure came to an end. I was reminded by the halfway house counselor that I was to report to my probation officer within three days of my release from the halfway house. In addition to my prison sentence, I was required to serve five years' supervise probation.

I continued working as an electrician and completed the course that allowed me to obtain a license journeyman electrician's. As I began to re-acclimate myself life, I saw some of my old friends during my daily travels back and forth to work. Some of them tried to encourage me to go back to selling drugs or to participate in other illegal activities. I refused to return to such a life. I would not hang out or associate with anyone I knew from the past. I was afraid of going back to prison. I kept my distance from anyone I'd associated with before going to prison. I **refused** to make the mistakes that I'd made in the past. I applied my will power to staying away from anyone who would place me on a path to return to prison. I'd learned from my mistakes, and I was determined not to repeat them. I would apply what I learned in prison to help me stay out of prison.

Chapter 14

Desire

When I was in prison I always dreamed of having a family and a house. I wanted to raise my kids and teach them all about the positive things in life. Most importantly, I wanted my kids to graduate from high school and college. Be careful for what you wish for in life.

One night, out of the blue, my brother called me around nine thirty. I reluctantly answered the phone. My brother informed me that he was at a friend's family party. My high school sweetheart was at the party, and she looked great. I told my brother that I was in for the night and did not feel like going to a party. My brother refused to accept no for an answer. He finally convinced me to go to the party. When I arrived, I looked across the room and saw my high school sweetheart, looking extremely beautiful. Our eyes locked, and we immediately walked toward each other and picked up where we'd left off in high school. I knew when I saw her that she would become my wife, and we would raise a family.

Within a year we were married and living in a one-bedroom apartment. I wanted to raise my family in a house and give my children the best opportunities to succeed in life. I began to work long hours. Before I knew it, I was working two jobs. A few months later I applied for a job as a union electrician. I was accepted and began working for an electrical company that primarily worked on multimillion-dollar homes located on the island of Palm Beach. I was exposed to the lifestyle of the rich and famous, though I never had an opportunity to meet any of the homeowners.

Things were beginning to move in a positive direction for my family and me. I worked on the island for four years, but I did not enjoy it. The homeowner in Palm Beach did not allow company employees to enter the residences through the front door, with the exception of new homes under construction. Workers were not allowed to use the same elevators as the owners; workers were required to use the service elevators. There were sound ordinances that restricted any type of noise before 10:00am in the morning. Although the job paid well, it was not fun.

One day I received a call from the union hall, informing me that there were high-paying job opportunities to working in other states. There was a shortages of experiencing electricians. I decided to take the union up on the offer.

My first job was in York, Pennsylvania. We were building a steel manufacturing plant for New York Steel. The project took one year to complete, and the pay was earning over $130,000 a year. Although we were paying living expenses in two states, we were able to save more with me working away from home. So when the project was completed in York, Pennsylvania. I began working at a chemical plant in Boston, Massachusetts. I worked at the chemical plant for two years. When the project was completed, I decided that I'd had enough of the road. It was time to return home.

During my time on the road, my wife and I purchased a duplex and a small home. We lived on one side of the duplex and rented the other apartment. Our plan was to demolish our small home and build a new home for my family. I had no experience building a home other than watching the process during my time on construction sites.

I returned home during a recession, and jobs were not available. The union was having a hard time keeping all the local union electrician employed. I decided to help a friend I knew who was a building contractor. When I approached the contractor and informed him that I wanted to offer my services to him for free, he asked me why I would do that. I explained that I wanted to gain experience in building homes industry. He smiled and told me that I would not make it in the industry with no experience. I told him that I would provide me service to his company free of charge. He informed me to be at his office the following Monday at eight.

I worked for the builder for nine months, approximately six to eight hours a day, five days a week. I gained a lot of experience from working with him. I learned how to build a house from the ground up. I learned how to schedule subcontractors, and I got some insight into how to run a construction company.

My wife and I began to design our home with an architect. Once the plans were completed, we began to look for financing from the major banks. I thought that obtaining the financing for our home would be the easy part. Low and behold, I was denied by all of the major banks. I turned to the community banks and credit unions to finance the new home, to no avail. Finally, after being rejected by twenty-nine lending institutions, my wife and I paid off our credit cards and one of our vehicles to reduce our debt-to-income ratio. Once the credit scores rose after our decreased debt was reflected on our credit report, we reapplied with Sterling Bank. One month later Sterling Bank approved the construction loan, and we began construction immediately.

I would not sleep for three and four days at a time while building our home. Once the foundation, walls, and roof were built, I began the electrical wiring for the house, one room at a time. Once I'd wired the house, I assisted the plumber and the air-conditioning subcontractors. The subcontractors always questioned why I was helping them to complete their job. My response was that I did not intend to pay the bank interest for fourteen months. I advised them that I would have this house completed within four to six months.

My wife was pregnant at the time. She was the material runner for the project. She was responsible for ordering and picking up the materials. My wife continued to run back and forth to Home Depot during the final days of the pregnancy. In the end, the house was finished in four months. My wife and I had our first child, and she was able to bring him home to our brand-new house. I was proud of myself. Because of my desire to want to have a family, God granted my wish. I sat on the front porch with my son, and I promised him that I would always be there to raise him. And I would never return to prison.

Building the house gave me the desire to become a general contractor. I woke up one morning and told my wife that I wanted to be a certified general contractor. My wife encouraged me to follow my dream and said that she would support me every step of the way. The next day I purchased all of the books and materials that were necessary to become a general contractor and signed up for classes, as well.

I visited from the builder I had helped. He offered me a job working for him as a foreman. The job would not pay as much as the union, however. I told him that I was grateful for the job opportunity, but I would need to speak to my wife prior to making a decision. My wife and I decided that it was in my best interest to continue working in the construction industry, would enable me to continue to gain knowledge and experience. I accepted the job.

While I was in prison, Russell and my mother had separated but did not divorce. My mother had retired from her job and spent her days alone in the house. I took my mother to work with me while visiting the jobsites. After a few weeks of riding around with me, my mother asked if she could care for our newborn instead of riding with me. My wife and I agreed to the offer, and Mother began to take care of Jordan.

Time went by. One day Mom called me and asked that I come to the house immediately. I was worried. I thought something had happened to Jordan. I didn't know what to think. My heart raced. I arrived at my mother's house and knocked on the door. Mother opened the door, and Jordan ran to me. I was confused and perplexed about why she'd required me to drop everything and come to her house. Mother then informed me that Russell had passed away from a heart attack. I cried for days and didn't speak to anyone.

A few weeks later, we buried Russell. Family members from across the United States attended the funeral. Russell's longtime girlfriend did not like the fact that my mother had all of the rights to his body. They were still legally married. Instead of burying Russell in Miami, where he had relocated, Mother buried Russell in West Palm Beach, where she, all of my siblings lived.

Six months later, I was in a large conference room in Orlando, taking the test to become a general contractor. I failed the forth part test by one point. Studying for the general contractor exam required me to study sixteen books. I failed the test because I was overconfident. I did not study as much as I should have and thought that I could spot-study and pass the test.

I was back in the same room four months later. I failed the test for the second time by nine points. I was very upset with myself because I knew why I hadn't passed the test. I had not studied as I should have studied. The next time around, I would not let the opportunity pass me by. I studied day in and day out. I didn't go out with the family or hang out with my brothers. I went to work during the day and studied at night. The third time I took the test, I finally passed it.

I had exhausted all of my resources while building our home. I went to my mother for funding to start Built Right Construction. My mother gave me all of her savings to start the company. I started a general contracting firm and began looking for work. Six months later I still hadn't landed my first project. I finally landed my job, a $1,200 project. The jobs continued to come in. The company grew beyond my wildest dreams, generating multimillion-dollar revenue within two years.

My wife began working for the company, and we continued to work together. I always said to her that I wanted to give back to the community. My wife and her brother Marcus started booking me for speaking engagements at schools, churches, and various community events. Some schools requested that I speak to all of the students in the school.

During the holidays, the church we attended assisted prisoners by providing gifts for their children. I claimed all of the tickets from the Christmas tree. Marcus and my wife, fulfilled their children's Christmas wishes. Marcus and I became close friends. When I was experiencing difficulties in life, I confided in Marcus. Marcus would tell me when he disagreed with me and didn't care how I felt when he was giving me good advice. We had a mutual understanding. Marcus and my mother were there for me from the inception of the new company.

I wanted to diversify the company and create a metal manufacturing division. Marcus was in charge of marketing for the company. He began to promote the metal manufacturing to various companies, distributors, and suppliers. The company had approximately thirty full-time employees. It looked as if everything was moving forward in the right direction.

Then the Great Recession came. Without any warning, our revenues decreased by 80 percent. The credit market began to freeze, as well. It looked as if the entire economy was about to fall off a cliff and send the United States into a depression.

Just when I thought things could not get any worse, my mother had a heart attack. She was rushed to the hospital. I visited my mother in the hospital daily. At one point the doctors did not think that my mother was going to survive. So I began to spend as much time as I could with my mother in the hospital. I did my work from the hospital so that I could remain close to her. She eventually recovered and was discharged. When mother was released, I felt as if a large rock was lifted from my shoulders. We had come close to mother passing away; I did not want to lose her.

I returned to work and continued the daily tasks of dealing with a bad economy. I had to make some tough business decisions. I reduced all of the employees' hours, returned half of the company vehicles to the dealer, and eliminated health insurance. In business school we were taught not to fraternize with employees. It is a rule I strongly recommend. One night my wife woke up and strongly suggested that I begin laying off employees.

The next morning, I had to lay off ten employees. A few weeks later, I laid off all the remaining employees. The office personnel had become the new work force. If the company was awarded any work, we would hire sub-contractors to complete the work.

As the weekend began, the business was all I could think about. My wife suggested that we find a movie on television. As I began searching channels, I received a phone call from my sister. She asked me to hurry to the house. I asked that someone called 911. My wife and I rushed next door to my mother's house. When I arrived, I sat down with my mother and tried to keep her calm. I saw that my mother could not breathe and it seemed as if the police or ambulance had not arrived. I asked my sister to call for the 911 again. All of a sudden my mother grabbed my hand, looked me in the eyes, and squeezed my hand with what I call the grip of death. As I realized that my mother was passing away, at the very last moment I pulled my hand away and the paramedics began to work on my mother. The paramedics spent forty-five minutes inside of the paramedic's front of my mother's home. Finally, the paramedics drove my mother to the hospital. The doctors tried to resuscitate her, to no avail. The doctor came out to speak to the entire family. He informed us that they were unsuccessful. He explained that my mother had passed away upon arrival at the hospital; the doctors did all that could be done. All of family was devastated by the news that Mother had passed away.

I did not speak to anyone for days. I could not bring myself to cry, because I was afraid I would not recover.

The family began to prepare for funeral. My mother wanted to be buried in a mausoleum. However, my stepfather was buried in a plot in the Memorial Gardens. I knew that my mother loved my father and would want to be buried next to him for eternity. I explained to the family that I wanted to pull my stepfather from his plot in the ground and place him in the mausoleum with my mother. The family agreed, and Russell's casket was removed from the plot and placed in the mausoleum. My mother's funeral was scheduled four days after the decision to move Russell. I asked the family to make sure that my mother had shoes on her feet and money and her driver's license in her purse. I wanted my mother to arrive at the church in a hearse and leave the church for the cemetery on a horse-drawn carriage.

People came from all over the United States to attend mother's funeral. There was standing room only at the service with and occupancy of 320. All of the former employees of the company attended as well. When the service concluded, I asked six of my former employees to carry my mother's body to the carriage. All of the company vehicles lined up behind the horse-drawn carriage, and the remaining vehicles followed behind the company vehicles. Traffic on both sides of the road stopped to allow the vehicles to pass through traffic.

Upon the pastor's last word, I asked the attendees who had grown up with us in Belle Glade to gather for a picture in front of the mausoleum. After the picture was taken, I asked all of the former employees to pose for a picture as well. Then the mausoleum was closed, and family and friends celebrated the life of mother at one of my sibling's home. I did my best to make sure that they all enjoyed themselves. When the night was over, I was yearning for mother. Mother was my friend, and she'd never turned her back on me. I could always count on my mother. Now she had passed away. I didn't know how to mourn her. I think about her daily, and she will always be dear to my heart.

I returned to work and reviewed the company's bank account. Both the company's and my personal resources were depleted. If I did not find a way to increase revenue, I would have to close the doors of the business. I remained upbeat, my attitude positive. At tax time I finally made it to my accountant's office to submit all of the required documentation for tax returns. My accountant informed me that one of his clients had recently sold his roofing company, but he did not want to retire. He explained that the client wanted to continue to work in the field of roofing. He asked if I would be interested in speaking to him. I told my accountant that I would speak or meet with him at his convenience.

A few days later, my accountant called and provided me with a phone number for a gentleman named Julius. I called him and introduced myself. We spoke for a couple of hours. Julius wanted to visit the office the next day. I gave him the address and directions to the office. The next day he arrived bright and early. Julius appeared to be in his late eighties. He was a white male, approximately five foot seven. He used a cane to assist him with his walking. I gave him a tour of the office and introduced him to the staff. When I introduced Julius to my wife, they developed an instant relationship. They spoke to each other for an hour as if I were not in the room.

Julius and I sat and talked for hours about the business. We spoke about what we felt was going wrong with the company and what would be required to get the company back on the right track. Julius requested a copy of the company's financials and profit-and-loss statements. He also requested a business plan, marketing materials, and a marketing plan. He asked that I bring all the information to his residence.

We spent hours going through the information. Julius asked me to explain the numbers within the reports. We got a chance to know each other. We went out to dinner that evening. We talked about life in general, allowing us the opportunity to get to know each other. When the day came to an end, I went home for the evening.

The next morning Julius called me at six o'clock and asked if I was at the office. I told him that I was on the way to the office. He said that he would meet me there in an hour. After Julius arrived at the office, he said he was going to show me how to take the company to another level. He suggested we expand the general contracting side of the business. He thought that the key to our future success would be to do more business with the federal government. I informed Julius that doing general contracting work for the federal government required a very high bonding capacity. I did not presently have the bonding capacity to take on that work. His response surprised me. Julius informed me that he would be willing to put up collateral. Julius told me that he would finance all future projects. He wanted to be involved in the bidding process from the beginning. He also wanted to see the bid and the budgets for all projects prior to funding the project.

He suggested that I contact bonding companies to obtain bonding. Bonding is required to perform construction work for projects over $200,000. Project bonds are issued by bonding agencies, which also set the bonding limits. Julius wanted the company to have the ability to perform two multimillion-dollar projects at the same time.

I finally found a bonding company that was willing to issue the company bonding capacity. The bonding company advised me that without Julius's collateral to back a five-million-dollar bond and a cashier's check for $250,000 made out to the bonding company, the bonding company would not be able to assist the company with bonding.

I was afraid to provide the information to Julius, in case he'd back out of the deal to help the company. When I called and told him about the requirements, Julius advised me to meet him at his house the following morning at nine o'clock. He also requested that I have the bonding company send a representative to meet with us there. The next morning I met Julius at his house. He met me in the parking lot and asked me to drive his vehicle to the bank. I drove him to the bank and waited for him in the lobby. Half an hour later, Julius returned and provided me with the check made out to the bonding company.

Julius insisted that I immediately begin bidding on government projects and that I personally read all of the bid documents. Once the bonding was secured, I began signing up with governmental agencies to bid on projects. We also signed up with Macy's, Walmart, Burger King, and McDonald's to renovate existing buildings or build new stores and restaurants. I personally met with representatives from the various entities.

Julius and I decided that Walmart would give us our best opportunity to land a multimillion-dollar project. Walmart required all firms to obtain umbrella insurance, company bonding capacity and to take several classes at Walmart's headquarters in Bentonville, Arkansas.

One year later, we were awarded our first Walmart project. We were responsible for remodeling 127,000 square feet Walmart store in Jupiter, Florida. Each night we were responsible for coordinating with Walmart staff for the removal of products from the shelves. This was accomplish by removal of the products off the shelves, remove and discard the shelves, remove the existing flooring, ceiling, and more. The walls were to be painted, and all of the products were to be restocked on the new shelves by 6:00 am each morning. New air-conditioning units were to be installed and the parking lot paved and striped. The store was completely remodeled in seventy-five days.

It looked as if things were turning around for the company. Walmart sponsored my attendance at a business course at Tuck University. The experience at Tuck School of Business opened my eyes to a new way of conducting business. After attending the class, I was featured in *Black Enterprise Magazine.*

Julius continued to fund projects from roofing and other construction projects. The city of Riviera Beach awarded us the contract to construct two residential homes after the Walmart projects. The homes were constructed in forty-five days. Julius funded the projects at zero interest.

The agreement with the City of Riviera Beach and the company was that upon the completion of the homes, the city would sell the homes to one of their pre-qualified buyer, the transaction to pay for the construction within sixty days. Eight months later, the City of Riviera Beach had no buyers for the new homes. We were forced to bring the issue to the city commissioner at a schedule meeting. In an effort to work things out with the city of Riviera Beach, we forfeited the profit to make the deal work.

After four months of placing bids on projects, we had only managed to come in second place on a couple of projects. Julius always asked me after each bid, "Did you understand the project? Did you provide the agency all of the required documents? Were you confident that you could complete the project and make a profit?" My response to all of the questions was yes. Then Julius advised me that I had done my job and not to be down on myself about the bad streak. I was frustrated by the fact that I had a golden opportunity with Julius as a financial backer, plus a substantial bonding capacity, and yet we could not get over the hump.

The economy began slowly recovering. I had to find a way out of my financial troubles. Julius continued to give me support and helped me cover some of the overhead through the tough times. One night Julius called me in the middle of the night and asked me when I was going to make a payment to him for the Walmart project. I was confused. I didn't know what to make of Julius's questions. I had already returned all of the funds that we'd borrowed from Julius for the Walmart project. I advised Julius that I would provide him with copies of the checks that were made out to him. I further explained that the checks had been cashed by him. Julius's informed me that he had no memory of the payments and asked if I would provide him with the copies of the checks. The next day I provided him with the copies as requested. Julius was satisfied with the canceled checks.

He also asked me to contact the bonding company and inform them that he wanted the collateral returned to him. Julius explained that collateral was required in the beginning to establish a relationship with the bonding company. He felt that I had proven myself and established a relationship with the bonding company, so the collateral should no longer be required. I contacted the bonding company and explained Julius's request for the return of the collateral and his reasoning. The bonding company agreed with Julius and had no issue with returning the collateral. However, the bonding company informed me that our bonding capacity would be reduced to one million dollars. I understood and agreed to the new terms. The collateral was returned to Julius. When the check from the bonding company cleared the bank was a relief for me. Although our bonding capacity was reduced, Julius and I were satisfied with our accomplishment of establishing a relationship with a bonding company that did not require me to use my personal home as collateral.

One evening Julius called and told me that he was lost. He began to ask me questions about different streets and cross sections. I asked him to let me come to him. We would leave the location together. He refused my help and told me that I did a great job of assisting him. I called him and asked him if I was welcome to visit him that night. Julius told me that I was always welcome at his house. On the drive down, I realized what was going on with Julius. Julius had dementia. I don't know why I was not able to detect it prior to that night. I picked up coffee and rang the doorbell. Julius opened the door and gave me a big hug. We sat down and talked for a couple of hours. There was no mention of the event from earlier in the day. Julius began to cry. He told me that his companion of nine years had passed away, and the funeral was scheduled for some time the following week. I asked him if I could accompany him to the funeral. Julius said he would love for me to do so.

During our three-year relationship, I did not have the chance to meet Julius's kids or family members. Julius shared that his daughter was due to arrive from New York to attend the funeral. The morning of the funeral I called Julius and asked him if he wanted me to drive him and his daughter to the funeral. Julius said that he was not handicapped and he would drive. I was to meet him at the chapel.

I was surprised by the cultural differences between this funeral and funerals I had attended in the past. For example, in my African American culture the men and boys wore three-piece suits, and the women and girls wore fancy dresses. We sang a lot of songs, and everyone had a chance to reflect on memories. Once the body was laid to rest, we gathered at one of the family member's homes or the church for a repast. Some family members wore T-shirts with pictures of the loved one on the front of the shirt.

My experience at this funeral felt odd. I wore a three-piece suit, and my wife wore a nice black dress. Most of the family members were dressed in shorts and T-shirts. Some family members wore blue jeans and a T-shirt. Besides me, the pastor was the only other person wearing a suit. No one sang any songs, and there were no speeches. Once the service concluded, we drove to the cemetery. Julius's companion's body was placed in a mausoleum with her husband. When the body was laid to rest, Julius and I sat there for a moment. Julius began to speak his last words to his longtime companion. He told her that he'd enjoyed her company and the time that they'd spent together.

We got up and left the cemetery and returned to the funeral home. My wife and I were the only African Americans in attendance. We could feel the tension and uncertainty in the room. I felt as if everyone in the room wanted to know how we'd become acquainted with Julius. As Julius and I moved about the room and then sat down, I could feel everyone looking at me. Julius's daughter asked him if he wanted something to eat, and he told her that he was not hungry. I waited a few minutes before asking Julius to at least have a sandwich and a drink. He asked me to get it for him. His daughter was not happy with that response. I finally asked Julius to introduce me to the individuals in the room. Julius began to introduce me to the family members as they came over to our table. When it was time to leave the funeral, Julius and his daughter were going back and forth about him driving home. I intervened and suggested to Julius that he allow his daughter to drive home and said I would follow them to the house. Julius agreed. We left the funeral home and drove to Julius's home. It was apparent that his daughter did not want us to come inside. Never in my wildest dreams would I have thought that I would never have a chance to see Julius again.

I returned home that afternoon feeling uncomfortable. The rest of the day did not go well for me. Around seven thirty that evening I called Julius. His daughter answered the phone and asked who was calling. When I told her my name, she hung up. I called back two days later, and she hung up again. When I called a few days later, a different woman answered the phone; she informed me that she was Julius' caretaker. She also informed me that Julius's son and daughter asked that I not call or visit the house.

Julius had always given me an open invitation to visit his home, and now I was being told that I was not welcome. During the time that I had spent with Julius, I had never seen any of his children or any of his immediate family visits him. It was always Julius and his companion. I knew that I had lost a friend. Although I was hurt, I had no other choice but to respect their wishes. After speaking to the caretaker, I never spoke to or saw Julius again.

Eight months later, I received a call from a former employee, who informed me that Julius had passed away. I asked him if he knew where he was going to be buried. He told me that he would try to obtain that information and get back to me. Two days later he called me and said that Julius had been buried. He did not know the burial site. I cried after I hung up. I kept wondering what I had done to Julius's children for them to not allow me to attend the funeral. Julius and I were friends. I should have been able to pay my last respects to the man who had taught me so much. I thought to myself, *I will always remember all of the good times that we experienced. I will forever be grateful to Julius; he will forever be in my heart.* Julius left a torch with me. Before I leave this earth, I pray that God will give me a chance to pass the torch to someone the same way Julius passed it to me. I love you, Julius.

Chapter 15

Courage

I realized an important lesson after Julius's passing. Russell had taught me as a child to work hard and to support my family. Julius taught me how to run a business and create opportunity to support my family. I learned from Julius the importance of people depending on you to get the job done. During the time that Julius had helped me establish the company as a general contractor, I had not generated enough profit to bring the company out of the red. I had to pick myself up and find a way to get back on my feet. I began to analyze the company. After careful consideration, I decided to shift the focus to the roofing division. The reason was simple; the operational costs to run the roofing division were extremely low as opposed to construction. The returns on the roofing division were higher than construction, and most roofing projects were completed in weeks, if not days. Most construction projects were completed within three to six months.

I created two additional businesses that failed within the first year. I do not allow character building moment in my life to define my future. Every failure in life has an equal potential for a new seed of success. There is no magic to becoming successful in life. As long as God wakes me up each morning and gives me an opportunity, I will continue to move in a forward direction. I will not allow my fears of my past failings to stop me from creating a business to support a quality lifestyle for my family. I will continue to have the courage to pursue my dreams. I will have the courage to succeed. Failure is not an option for me; I have too many people depending on me. In life, we have to learn from our past misfortunes and continue to plant new seeds of success. I have a burning desire to become successful in life, and I have faith in God that I will overcome temporary setbacks. I will not quit until I succeed.

Chapter 16

Imprison the Mind

Do not waste any time or energy concerning yourself with where you are in life at this point. Your life is working. It does not matter if you are incarcerated, a convicted felon, poor, or living on the streets. It doesn't matter if you do not have any money, are in a rehab facility for drugs, if you've lost your mother or father, are divorced, lost your job or did not get that promotion to a become partner in the law firm. It doesn't matter if you are rehabbing from an accident or if the doctor has given you some bad news, if you live in a foster home or are being raised by your grandmother, if you filed for bankruptcy or experienced any other temporary setback. *Look up and get up*!

When I first placed my feet on prison ground for the very first time, I made my mind up that I was not ever going back to prison. I was determined to overcome that temporary setback. *I immediately took responsibility for my actions.* I began examining all of the reasons and bad decisions that led me to prison. I stop blaming everyone else for my failures and continued taking responsible for my bad actions. Then I began telling myself that everything was my fault. I also made a commitment that for the rest of my life I would look for fault in all situations. What do I mean? If you are in line and someone skips ahead of you, do not approach to show the person to the end of the line. Instead, smile and kindly inform the person in charge of the issue. Stay focused on the reason you are there. Maybe you did not close the gap in the line because you were on your cell phone or reading a book.

I began taking blame for everything. If someone was one hour late to a meeting, I took blame for it. It was my fault that he or she was late. I should have reconfirmed the appointment. When you assume the blame for everything, you immediately shut down your negative thoughts or emotions. When you are able to master this technique, you will see your life change in a positive way. You will find yourself feeling happy, with increased energy. You will feel invincible, like you can accomplish anything.

I want to teach you how to imprison the mind, how to overcome the challenges that you face. I defied the odds of succeeding. From that moment on, I made my mind up that I would no longer make excuses. I would no longer complain or say it was someone else's fault. I would no longer worship the problem. I made up my mind up that I would no longer be a victim and let things continue to happen to me. I would begin to create new opportunities for myself. I would no longer make excuses for anything.

No more excuses. Let's get to work. The first thing that you have to decide is what you want to accomplish in the next 30 days, 60 days, 90 days, 120 days 180 days, 270 days, and 360 days.

You have three minutes to answer the following questions. Don't think. Just answer the questions.

1. What do you want to accomplish in this lifetime?

   _____

   _____

   _____

2. What do you want to be (doctor, entrepreneur, president)?

   _____

   _____

3. How much money do you want to make a year?

   _____

   _____

4. What are your goals and dreams?
   A. _____
   B. _____
   C. _____
   D. _____
   E. _____
   F. _____
   G. _____

Make a commitment to write down your goals and dreams on a daily basis, morning and night. Do not concern yourself with how you will accomplish these goals and dreams at this time. Your brain will do that for you automatically. You can program your brain to find ways to prioritize and organize your goals and dreams. Your brain will automatically navigate you in the right direction to accomplish your goals and dreams.

Some have said that the human brain functions like a homing pigeon. Take a homing pigeon out of their current location. You may place the homing pigeon in a cage and cover the cage with a couple of dark blankets. Place the homing pigeon in the cage in a dark van. Drive twelve hundred miles in any direction. Open the cage and release the homing pigeon. The homing pigeon would fly in the sky and make three circles in the air. After gathering coordinates, the homing pigeon will then fly back to the original location where the journey began. Help your brain accomplish your goals and dreams the same way by writing down your goals and dreams daily. Write them down the first thing in the morning when you awaken and before bedtime.

Wake up one or two hours before your regular time to wake up. If you normally wake up at six thirty to get ready for work and help the kids off to school. Wake up one hour early, wake up at five. After writing down your goals, spend the next hour reading anything about your craft. If you are a teacher, read information that enhances your teaching abilities. If you are a car mechanic, read about new techniques or technologies. If you just got out of prison and want to own your own business, read or listen to books on how to start and successfully run a business. Do not read any book until you read *#1New Your Times*

Bestseller Tony Robbins book "Money Master The Game, 7 simple steps to financial freedom" If you are a divorced woman and have never worked outside the home, read or listen to books related to women bouncing back on their feet. Listen to motivational speakers or buy their videos. *Read Grow Your Value by Mika Brzezinski.* Learn how to type or how to use Excel spreadsheets, or read books about how to become an entrepreneur. I recommend reading or listening to *The Closer's Survival Guide, Third Edition* by Grant Cardone or *Close That Sale* by Brian Tracy. Spend the first hour of each day improving you. Find a comfortable chair, and for the next fifteen minutes close your eyes and begin focusing on your breathing. Breathe in slowly. Breathe in and breathe out. For the next fifteen minutes just take deep breaths and exhale slowly.

How did that feel? Do this for the next thirty days. If possible, meditate at in the same place and time every morning. Master these skills, and watch your life change. I recommend reading *The Miracle Morning* by Hal Elrod or *The Miracle of Self-Discipline* by Brian Tracy.

The next phase of the transformation is to stop watching television or listening to the radio. In order for you to make a total life transformation, you must control what you are feeding the mind. For example, instead of feeding your mind with what time your favorite TV or radio shows, begin feeding your brain new information. You have to read *The Power of Your Mind by John Kehoe.* You have to feed the mind new information as if your life is at stake. Listening to books during the course of your day. Listen to books in the car, at the office, and at home. Listen to books while you are taking your morning run or your afternoon walk. Read or listen to motivational books. Remember, the brain functions like a homing pigeon. I recommend reading or listening to *Rewire - Change Your Brain* by Richard O'Connor, *The 10X Rule* by Grant Cardone, *The E Myth Revisited* by Michael E. Gerber, *How They Did It* by Robert Jordan, *905 to Rio* by Evans MacDowell, or one of my favorite books, *A Whole New Mind* by Daniel Pink.

Take charge of what you feed your body. It is extremely important that you drink plenty of water. Drinking a cup of lemon water first thing in the morning will help improve your heath. Cut a lemon in half and squeeze one half into a glass if you are 150 pounds and under. Use the whole lemon if you are 151 pounds or more. Add a full cup of water to the glass. Drink the lemon water. Do not concern yourself with the taste. Lemons are high in potassium, which is good for heart health, as well as brain and nerve function. Lemon juice provides your body with energy and reduces anxiety and depression. Lemon water is packed with vitamin C, which helps boost the immune system. Drinking lemon water helps flush out the toxins in your body by enhancing enzyme function, stimulating your liver. Believe it or not, drinking lemon water will help you lose weight. Drinking warm lemon water is the most effective way to reduce viral infections.

Stay away from flour products, and cut back on bread products. I do not eat at inexpensive fast food restaurants. Eat at quality restaurants. I encourage you to eat fruits, vegetables, and salads with every meal. Try to eat six to eight times a day. Eat your last meal around seven in the evening and have fruit for the remainder of the evening.

After you wake, meditate and drink a glass of lemon water (cold or warm). Go for a run or walk to clear your mind as you prepare to start your day. Twenty percent of your daily activity will produce 80 percent of your daily results. As you walk or run, think about what activity will produce the greatest results. Begin thinking of ways to improve these results. After your run or walk, write your ideas down on a piece of paper. Then write down the tasks that you need to complete by the end of the day. Scan and prioritize the list. Look for the task or assignment that will help you achieve the greatest result. Once you have identified that task, begin working on that task immediately. Do not stop or allow interruptions until that task is completed. Repeat this process until you have completed every task on your list for the day.

As you continue to practice these good habits, your brain will become stronger. Within four days, your brain will retain the new information. Once your brain finds the answer, it will alert you the solutions to you. Continue this process for thirty days. Your new habits will change your life. People will begin to see you differently.

Your friends and family will begin noticing the changes in you as well. Stay humble. Do not allow early successes to derail your focus. It is important that you stay disciplined.

Go to sleep early. Going to sleep between nine and ten at night will give you the energy to wake up early. Be careful not to eat any meals after eight at night. Eating after eight will make it more difficult to wake up in the morning with a burst of energy. I recommend reading or listening to *Make Yourself Unforgettable* by the Dale Carnegie Organization, *Six Months to Six Figures* by Peter J. Voogd, *How to Win Friends and Influence People* by Dale Carnegie. A must-read is *The Millionaire Next Door* by Thomas J. Stanley.

Chapter 17

Action Plan

1. Prepare a glass of lemon water. Set your alarm clock for 4:00 a.m. and go to bed early. Try your best to turn in for the night around ten.

2. When you wake up in the morning, drink your glass of lemon water and write down your goals and dreams.

3. Go for a run or walk.

4. Mediate for ten to fifteen minutes in the beginning. The goal is to mediate for thirty to sixty minutes every morning.

5. Read or listen to books pertaining to your trade or craft for forty-five minutes. You may also use this time to learn about a job or position you want in the future.

6. Arrive at work thirty minutes early. If you are in school or an athlete, that means arriving at school, the gym, or the practice facility thirty minutes early. Get a jump-start on your day. Write down every task that needs to be completed for the week. Then, prioritize the work that has deadlines and organize the list. Prioritize the work that will help the management team or head coach to be more successful. This is not the time to be concerned with individual accomplishment, only team accomplishment.

   This is not the time for you to concern yourself with how hard a classmate is working. When you are at school or in the classroom, do not spend time passing notes, reading material that is not related to the class subject, or playing around on the phone. Learn. Feed your mind while you are in school. Value this time, because you have only one high school life experience. It is important that you expand your mind. So when you are in school, give 130 percent of yourself in class. Make it a habit to turn in your homework or essay two days early. Use the extra time to expand your mind. Focus on what the teacher is teaching. Do what is best for you in each and every classroom. Do what is best for the team or company. When you are in a classroom, learn all that you can learn. Give your brain 130 percent of you. Value the information or the subject matter that you are feeding your brain. Complete all of the class assignments, and ask your teacher to suggest the books that he or she is reading to enhance your knowledge of the subject. Do what the coach asks of you without any complaining.

When you arrive at work, tell yourself you love your company and do everything in your power to help the company to be successful. You are at work to do one thing: work and do what is best for the company. Challenge yourself to give a 130 percent. Use the phone for emergency purposes only. Be disciplined and work the entire time you are at work. Do not text during working hours or while you are in school. I find it so disrespectful when I go to a bank and the teller is texting while he or she is taking care of my bank transaction. Do not let this happen to you.

Eliminate these bad habits and give a 130 percent of yourself. Dominate all aspects of your life. When someone tries to distract you, say you would love to help them with their concerns or issues. However, you have an important assignment that is due in two days. It is important task for the boss and it has to be done. Immediately return to studying, working, working on your goals, etc. Continue working on the most important task, to completion. The secret is working on one thing at a time until the task is complete. On Wednesday morning *this week*, I want you to walk into your classroom, coach's office, or supervisor or manager's office. Tell him or her that you have completed all of you tasks for the week and *you need more responsibility.* Tell your teacher or the head coach that *you want more responsibility.* Whatever additional class assignment that the teacher or additional drills that the coach asks you to do, or an additional assignment from your supervisor or manager, *immediately* begin working on the task until it is completed. Upon completion of the assignment, ask your teacher, coach, supervisor, or manager for *more responsibility. It is important to do this exercise for a period of thirty days.*

7. Plan your family activities so that you can take classes or study hall for an extra thirty minutes in school. Plan your family activities so that you can stay on the field, at the gym, or at work for an additional thirty minutes to one hour after everyone else is leaving for the day. Plan your family activities so that you can continue to practice sports skills. Get a jump on your homework or essay. Get a jump on the work that coach wants you to accomplish for the week. Get a jump on the assignment that would meet your supervisor or manager's goals for the week. Learn when you are in school, and read as many books a week as possible everyday of your life. Work on your game when you are practicing. Practice your techniques and master your craft. Catch more balls. Shoot more shots. Improve yourself.

When your mind tries to give you an excuse, when your mind tries to get you to cheat on your homework, tell yourself that it is important that you learn the class material. It is important for you not to cheat. Tell yourself that it is important that you study this class assignment because your life depends on it. Tell yourself that it is important to your team that you continue to practice. It is important that you continue to work because your team is counting on you. Your mother and father are counting on you. Your wife and kids are counting on you. Tell your mind, "No more excuses. Get back to work."

8. Read or listen to books pertaining to your trade or craft for forty-five minutes a day. You may also use this time to learn more about a job or position you want in the future.

9. Write down your goals and dreams at the end of your evening. Reflect on your goals. Think about all the positive things that you accomplished today. Tell yourself that you will improve on them tomorrow.

10. Spend 15-30 minute a day thing of five ideas. Write down these ideas on paper and compare your new ideas to the old ones. 90% of your ideas will be of no use. The other 10% has great potential to become the million dollar idea. It only takes one good idea to make you financial independent.

11. Prepare a glass of lemon water. Set your alarm clock for 4:00 a.m. and go to bed early. Try your best to turn in for the night around ten.

Let's summarize the action plan. If you discipline and condition your brain to follow this plan, you will accomplish the following:

1. Your GPA will improve by one to two points. You may end up with a 4.0 GPA.
2. Your football play will improve by 20 percent. Your basketball play will improve 20 percent. Your income will increase 30 percent.
3. You will condition your mind to start and finish to completion one thing at a time.
4. If you read for forty-five minutes in the morning and at night for a period of one year, is equivalent to you reading forty to fifty books a year.
5. You will have trained your brain to have tremendous amounts of muscle power.
6. You will have been promoted in your job or will soon be promoted.
7. Some of you will become entrepreneurs and start you own company or companies.

8. You will improve the quality of your life and your health.
9. You will have total control of your emotions.
10. You will have trained yourself in the habits that have made the top 20 percent of Americans successful.
11. You will have eradicated excuses and procrastination and overcome your fear of failure.
12. You will have trained yourself to be successful.

I was forced to use this plan when I was in incarcerated. I was forced to reeducate myself. I was forced to be disciplined. I had no choice. I was told when I could take a shower, when I was allowed to eat or go to the gym. The prison decided when I was able to go the library. Although the prison had total control over where I was housed and total control of my movements. The prison system had no control of my mind. The prison system did not control what I did with my free time. I took personal responsibility for my life. I took control of what I fed my body. I was determined to succeed. Within the first year after being released, I was earning $80,000 a year. After being on the job for three years, I was earning $120,000.

I challenge you to give this plan 130 percent. This plan has helped me to give myself and my resources back to my community. This plan helped me to start a family and then raise four kids. I married my lovely wife because of this plan. I am in love with my kids, and they are in love with me because of this plan. I created a successful construction and roofing company, with no knowledge of the industry, because of this plan. I created a successful construction company, with no knowledge of the industry, because of this plan. The company's largest project to date was the complete renovation of Walmart for $2.4 million. This plan has helped me to earn a multimillion-dollar contract with the School District of Palm Beach County. I am happy with what I have given back to my community because of this plan. I am in a happy place in my life because of this plan. To further enrich your mind, I recommend that you read *The Thirty-Three Strategies of War, The Art of Seduction,* or *48 Laws of Power,* all by Robert Greene, *The Secret to Success by Eric Thomas and Greatness Is Upon You: Laying the Foundation by Eric Thomas*

I offer this plan to you. Use this plan to improve the quality of your life and ultimately to live life in abundance. You owe it to yourself to take personal responsiblity of your life. If a high school dropout can turn his life around, you can do it. Take control of your life and begin living out your goals and dreams.

A Word from the Author

In life, you cannot simply desire success. You must have a plan of action to achieve success. Now you have a plan. If you stay on this plan for a ten-year period, you will have improved your life by 1,000 percent. It will take 10,000 hours to master a new craft. I have no hard feelings that I had to start over. I relish the opportunity. I learned from my experiences of being incarcerated and overcoming temporary setbacks. I learned from the lessons taught to me by my mother, Russell, and Julius. Now I want to become a motivational speaker and give back to the prison system. I want to help prison tap within their greatness and improve their life prior to being release from prison. I want to speak to professional businesses and at public and private events. I want to speak to professional basketball and football teams. I will continue speaking to children throughout the communities in the United States and internationally. I will continue giving back to the community and making the world a better place. I want to be remembered as a person who helped to make a difference in this world.

If you take anything from this book, please learn from my mistakes, it is too costly learning from you own mistakes. Imprison your mind and follow the action plan. Surround yourself with positive people who will encourage your dream and challenge you to accomplish your goals. Read as many books as possible. Do not let temporary setbacks discourage you. When things do not turn out the way you expected, or when you fail, you have to find a way to continue. Do not give up! Keep fighting every day, working toward your goals and dreams. Plan for your success, and execute the plan. Good luck!

For booking, mentoring, parties, and speaking engagements, call (561) 723-6775 or e-mail itstimemsi@gmail.com.

E-mail your positive experiences.

Sincerely,
Hydn Rousseau